THE TRANSFORMATION OF

AMERICAN CATHOLIC SISTERS

IN THE SERIES

WOMEN IN THE POLITICAL ECONOMY,
edited by Ronnie J. Steinberg

THE TRANSFORMATION OF

AMERICAN CATHOLIC SISTERS

Lora Ann Quiñonez, CDP, and
Mary Daniel Turner, SNDdeN

Temple University Press
Philadelphia

Temple University Press, Philadelphia 19122
Copyright © 1992 by Temple University. All rights reserved
Published 1992
Printed in the United States of America

Library of Congress Cataloging-in-Publication Data
Quiñonez, Lora Ann.
The transformation of American Catholic sisters / Lora Ann Quiñonez and
Mary Daniel Turner.
    p.   cm. — (Women in the political economy)
Includes bibliographical references and index.
ISBN 0-87722-865-5 (alk. paper)
    1. Monasticism and religious orders for women—United States—History—
20th century.   2. Nuns—United States.   I. Turner, Mary Daniel, 1925–
II. Title.   III. Series.
BX4220.U6Q56   1992
271'.90073'09045—dc20   91-11890

Contents

Preface

THIS IS A BOOK about change and about people changing. It is a book about women, American Catholic sisters, in passage. It tells of the radical transformation that has been underway among sisters for the past four decades, redefining their identities and their way of life.

Although new currents were stirring in the fifties, it is the twenty-five years since Vatican Council II that brought drastic changes in the personal and corporate lives of sisters, their institutions and ministries, their relations with laity, clergy, and hierarchy, their presence in the public sphere. Another, less obvious, change has also been in progress, a reformulation of *belief* about the meaning of religious life. This transformation is the result of deliberate efforts, collaborative by choice, of sisters to identify a core of shared faith that gives meaning and coherence to the highly diverse experiences and forms of religious commitment.

Sisters are a mere fraction of the American people, but the issues of their changing are far from esoteric. Their story is set within the larger story of the Catholic church, particularly since the mid-sixties, when Vatican Council II laid the theological groundwork for an ambitious task. Nothing less than total renewal would make the church a vital presence to contemporary peoples. No one took the mandate for renewal more seriously than the sisters. And no one was better positioned to tackle renewal purposefully than American sisters, to whom the previous decade had brought mammoth advances in higher education and the organization of critical national networks. They had, actually, over ten years' head start in developing the resources required for critical change.

Nor is the story of the sisters without vital links to the vast social transformation of American (and global) society since World War II. Without doubt, specific events and movements impacted the sisters—the awakening of the poor in Central America, the civil rights struggles of the sixties, and the flourishing of women's movements. And the questions sisters struggle with as they change are the same questions that have come with and from the experience of changing around the world. The energies and skills of the sisters have been galvanized by issues like the nature of religious identity and commitment, the link between religious affiliation and public involvement, the tensions between deliberate self-identification as women and participation in structures that deny women identity and exclude them from power, and the nature of conflict within and with institutions. We would argue that what has preoccupied American nuns in the period from 1950 to the present has import beyond the tens of thousands of women who have been the primary actors in the process. We think this story needs telling forthrightly, critically, and with love.

For some years the two of us talked sporadically about undertaking the task. It seemed to us that the record would add to knowledge about American religious thought, women's part in the making of the American people, institutional change, and the American Catholic church during a time of unusual ferment. Very little published research exists on the process of change experienced by American sisters collectively since mid-century. While comprehensive histories of American Catholicism have appeared in recent years (Jay Dolan, *The American Catholic Experience* [Garden City, N.Y.: Doubleday, 1985], and James Hennesey, *American Catholics* [New York: Oxford University Press, 1981], for example), they contain scant reference to sisters and do not focus on the process of the past few decades. Existing doctoral dissertations, finely limited in scope, do not seek a comprehensive overview. The portrayal of the changing sister in the popular media tends toward stereotype. Official church documents on religious life in the years since the Council are generalized elaborations of principle. They do not mirror the conditions of particular nations and cultures.

No single account is capable of encompassing the whole story. To make the project manageable, we chose to view the story through a particular lens, the Leadership Conference of Women Religious of the USA (LCWR). Founded in 1956, the Conference is a national association of the chief governing officers of American religious communities involved in active ministry (as distinct from cloistered groups). The thirty-plus years of the Conference's existence coincide with a major transitional period in society, church, and religious communities. Whether one celebrates or deplores the fact, it is widely acknowledged that the LCWR has been a force in the transformation process.

It is not the only lens we could have chosen. It is, however, a uniquely advantageous one. It is, first, a legally constituted moral person within the Catholic church with official status as a national conference of heads of orders. Second, its members come from the designated leadership of over 90 percent of the women's religious communities in this country. The Conference, then, is made up of women whose role exacts of them a certain preoccupation with issues of identity, meaning, and ultimate direction. It is the explicit business of the Conference to attend to the life and mission of sisters and to any conditions affecting them. Joining together in the LCWR, these women become a corporate body with a privileged vantage point from which to analyze common issues and devise common responses.

Are the women of the LCWR representative of American sisters? Is their experience typical? Are our conclusions about the transformation of sisters, based on the records of the LCWR, valid? Members of the hierarchy, Vatican and American, are given to undercutting the stands and orientations of the Conference by insisting that they are not. Sisters who approach change more conservatively accuse the LCWR of being "radical" and others, more militant perhaps, charge it with undue timidity, even downright co-optation by the institutional status quo. However, comparative studies of two ideologically opposed groups of community officers conducted by sociologist Marie Augusta Neal, SNDdeN, in the late sixties showed a high correlation between the beliefs of members and leaders in religious communities of women. At the same time, findings of the 1967 Sisters' Survey (a total population study conducted by the Conference) suggested that three groups within American communities had a stronger orientation toward change—the leadership, the women in charge of initiating new members, and the younger members themselves. The fact is that American sisters are not a monolithic group. The fact is, also, that both the original Sisters' Survey and a 1980 restudy of a random sample of sisters support the conclusion that, despite great diversity among communities and individuals, certain trends appear to be widely generalized.

The story of American sisters in passage is not a story about *those* women. It is *our* story as well. We are both members of religious communities. Our membership had its beginnings in "the old days," prior to Vatican II. We have known the former ways and shared in the making of new ones. We sense that a sorting out of the experience of change and what we have changed into might be useful for us as American sisters at this time.

We are insiders to the LCWR as well. Both of us were members of the Conference; both served on its governance bodies. Both of us held the post of executive director (Mary Daniel 1972–78, Lora Ann 1978–86). We were involved firsthand in a good number of the events the book tells about, sometimes as close observers, often as participants.

We bring certain biases to the work. For years our work offered us the immense privilege of journeying with American sisters, communities, and organizations in their post-

Vatican II experiences. We had opportunities to share learning with sisters from Europe, Asia, Africa, Canada, and South
and Central America. We have been touched by scores of
bright, gifted women for whom search has become a way of
life. We give their perceptions an honored place as a source
of knowledge. Both of us are feminists. That is, we take the
experience of women seriously as a place where truth can be
known; we categorically reject as unjust (and, therefore, sinful) the exclusion and diminishment of women whatever the
ideology used to validate such action; and we are committed
to the processes of awakening and empowerment through
which women are claiming themselves. Both of us believe the
transformation of religious life and of definitions of identity
among sisters is a positive movement.

We could have written this account of the movement of
transformation as a personal narrative. We chose not to. It
seemed to us that if we could combine the immediacy of
firsthand involvement and the distance of research, the work
would be richer. We wanted to take advantage of the insider's
access to the experience of these years—to the sensory and
emotional texture and to the intellectual comprehending-on-
the-spot of happenings and situations. We also wanted the
discipline of stepping back afforded by the study of sources.
So we set out to immerse ourselves in the history of the organization preserved in its written records and in the memories
of oral history informants. Some of the material in the book we
know because we were there. We participated in the events;
we heard and saw the people. The written records and the
oral history accounts were sources of both information and
validation.

Our starting point was a broad question—What are major
driving forces that have directed the change in the way American sisters understand and define religious life, commitment,
and ministry? Because we thought it important to allow the
answers to emerge from the sources, we did not start with

even tentative responses or categories. Only after a first immersion in written and oral sources did we begin to make notes of recurring themes to focus the study. These were refined and redirected several times before we completed our research.

From the beginning, then, we sought to work inductively. We also determined to work collaboratively. We talked to persons competent in American history, American Catholicism, theology, sociology, and oral history. Three times we invited a group of sisters (different in each case) to reflect with us on specific questions.

Our work together was an energetic and respectful partnership from the very beginning. We searched archival files in tandem. Frequent conversations marked every stage of the archival research and of the oral history interviews. Intermediate and final analyses were structured almost as two-person seminars, each of us writing brief pieces in response to questions framed by us and then discussing these. More challenging still, we co-authored the book. In the process we evolved (and continually refined) a method of prewriting each chapter in several stages. Working individually, both of us wrote an initial piece on our understanding of the topic, then a lengthy essay we came to dub affectionately a "wrt" (writing in order to think) in which we laid out what we knew and thought about the topic, and, finally, a description of what the chapter might look like, what ideas it should incorporate, and how it might be structured. We would present our writings to each other and thrash them out, seminar style. More than once our joint probings gave birth to new insights, truly the offspring of both. By the time we were ready to write a chapter, we had created its thought and structure jointly. Each chapter was written by one of us and each chapter is truly the work of both.

Our book is about new directions among American sisters in "apostolic" women's communities. Largely a product of the nineteenth and twentieth centuries, such communities arose to address human needs through active ministries. When we speak of the changing of "American sisters," we do not claim that our conclusions apply to every sister in this country or even, in some cases, a numerical majority. We cite new directions in definitions of identity and mission. The choice of categories to organize our findings is ours, but they are clearly based in the records.

One final note: language. It came as no surprise to us that in a time of radical change, experience outstrips words. Both of us believe that choosing what to name something or someone is no trivial pursuit. Words not only reflect experience, they fashion it as well. Language can support or block change. And when part of what is changing is a dominant worldview that underpins the structures of society, polity, religion, even epistemology, more than a little energy is poured into advocating or resisting new namings. So we wrestled often with how to label experiences described in this book. Sometimes we stumbled upon a happy solution; other times we declared a truce, knowing that change is not ended and language is being created.

One of our first naming problems was how to refer to the heroines of the story. "Nuns"? "Women religious"? "Religious"? (The use of this adjective as a noun is traditional.) "Vowed women"? In the end we fell back on "sisters," though occasionally we resort to one of the others. It is less cumbersome than some, less contested than others, and it is widely recognized by Catholic and non-Catholic. We also decided to use the term "American" to signify "of the United States," despite our appreciation of the argument that this usage is evidence of our national arrogance. There is no convenient equivalent, in our speech, for words deriving from the name of the country (like "Canadian," "German," "Israeli"). Historically the people of the United States refer to themselves and are referred to by many others as "Americans."

No book is complete without a section, however brief, headed "acknowledgments." And with good reason. No book comes to be except with the time and talents, freely shared, of many besides the author.

Our communities, the Sisters of Divine Providence and the Sisters of Notre Dame de Namur, have been supportive. Grants and contributions from the Lilly Endowment and twenty-five religious communities funded the archival research, oral history interviews, and consultations for the book. Those grants made possible the luxury of two years devoted exclusively to researching, writing, and thinking. Vincent Cushing, OFM, president of Washington Theological Union, was invaluable in drafting the grant proposal, giving us time and advice and enlisting the grant-writing expertise of Mary Holland as a resource. The executive committee of the LCWR encouraged our work, granting us full access to the archives and files of the conference. The staff of the Notre Dame University Archives, where the LCWR's archival records are deposited, were unfailingly helpful. During the ten weeks we camped among them, they took us in warmly, sharing even their bottomless coffee pot. The archivists of several religious communities—the Dominican Sisters (Adrian, Mich.), the Sisters of Charity of the Blessed Virgin Mary (Dubuque, Iowa), the Sisters of Loretto (Nerinx, Ky.), the Sisters of St. Joseph of Chestnut Hill (Pa.), and the Sisters Servants of the Immaculate Heart of Mary (Monroe, Mich.)—were marvelous to us. They cheerfully dragged out every box we requested, called our attention to other treasures, made sure we got to the dining room on time, and saw to it that we never ran out of pencils. Several communities extended gracious hospitality when we were working in archives or conducting interviews. With two exceptions, every person we asked for an interview not only said yes but gave us as much time as we wanted. Every one lavished energy and thought on preparing for the interview, sharing insights, and reviewing the written transcription. And through it all they made us feel as if we were doing them a favor! Over and over we rediscovered what we have long known—these women are truly sisters. Irene Harvey converted miles of tape into reams of paper, transcribing all the oral history interviews and revising them after the informants had examined them. Several readers gave us helpful feedback at various stages in our writing. Michael Ames at Temple University Press raised thoughtful questions that sent us back to the manuscript not merely to revise but to bring to light possibilities we had overlooked. As a result, the book grew toward its own integrity.

THE TRANSFORMATION OF

AMERICAN CATHOLIC SISTERS

Chapter One / Changing Times

"CHANGE" WAS HARDLY A BYWORD of the American Catholic church in the first half of this century. In the popular mind the church probably seemed an ancient behemoth given to alien ways, eternally on guard against incursions of secular culture. But nothing alive ever manages to escape change altogether. The fact is that the church was changing, of necessity, from the moment its transplanting to this land presented it with new realities. After World War II seminal changes occurred in its internal life—in biblical studies, in worship, in lay social action—whose full impact would be felt in a later age. But they went largely unremarked by the American public, and even Catholics did not experience them as significant alterations of Catholic identity.

Then, in 1958, John XXIII succeeded to the papacy. An uncontroversial, amiable compromise, whose election postponed the showdown between those who favored the status quo and those who understood that the church had some major changes to tackle, the man defied predictions. He promptly announced an ecumenical council in which all Catholic bishops were to participate. Before the Second Vatican Council ended, prominent non-Catholics as well as a smattering of Catholics (including women) had sat in as guest auditors. And an array of the church's most brilliant contemporary theologians, acting as official consultants to individual bishops or national groupings of them, had used their scholarship to give a highly intellectual cast to the ferment.

Vatican Council II held four sessions from 1962 to 1965. Its agenda covered a wide range—the nature and mission of the church; its relation to contemporary secular society as well as to other religions (Christian and non-Christian); the meaning of commitment in lay life, religious communities, and the priesthood; the sources of revelation; religious freedom; worship; education; and modern communications. As its members probed these fields, they touched, however lightly, on themes like the status of women in the church and the influence of culture on religious forms. Not then pursued in depth, these themes lay scattered throughout the Council's major statements waiting to be discovered by readers of every ideological stripe. In all, the Council produced sixteen official documents.

Twenty other councils (by the count of Western Catholicism) had preceded it; the last, Vatican I (1869–70), was of interest primarily to scholars of papal infallibility. Vatican II was the first council convened after the advent of electronic mass media. Its agenda was audacious. Quite simply it undertook to lay out the direction for the reform and renewal of the Catholic church *in the context of the contemporary condition.* In short order Vatican II wrought a clear mandate for change—substantive change. In fact, the Council itself mirrored the change already in process. As captured by the media, television in particular, the Council imaged a church even Catholics had not been aware of—a world church headed by bishops of different colors and languages, manifesting as much ideological diversity as any civil society. Their concerns were as plural as the cultures from which they came. They dared to dismember the working papers drafted by the preparatory commissions, demanding to elaborate totally new ones. They voiced divergent perceptions of God and the church and revelation and "the world." They even squabbled among themselves and took pot shots at one another's ideas through well-placed leaks. Through it all, in official assemblies and coffee bars and press briefings, they waxed earnest on the changes the church must make if it was to be a credible player in contemporary society. And it was very clear that the Council bishops believed the Roman Catholic church should participate in the making of contemporary history.

That Catholicism could change was as much a revelation to Catholics as it was to the public at large. Traditional instruction had emphasized that "the Church is unchangeable." (Since it already possessed all truth, change could only represent deviance or deterioration.) Generations of American Catholics grew up thinking that the way things were was the way things *are*. Now the official rulers and teachers spoke and acted a different message. Large numbers of American Catholics were exhilarated by the new insights about what the church might become. The spectacle of the Council showed them that diversity and Catholicism are not mutually exclusive. They began to think and talk about change. By the time the Council ended, many were primed for radical alteration in their ways of believing and worshiping and being governed. (Many were equally primed to resist and block change.)

The deliberate embarking by an entire church on a process of renewal (and hence on cataclysmic change) was an intriguing spectacle. During and just after Vatican II, the Roman Catholic church became a major feature of the evening news. American Catholics found themselves in the limelight, the attention of their fellow Americans riveted on them. Influential spokespersons in religious and civic arenas remarked with obvious approval on the anticipated change. Non-Catholics were actually speaking with affection about a pope! From being an alien, often suspect, minority in the land, American Catholics had become an interesting species, the subject of popular report and mass commentary.

If Catholics in general were an interesting lot, one group among them seemed to fascinate the public. The mysterious women whom ordinary usage named "sisters" or "nuns" suddenly emerged into the public eye. They appeared in "normal" clothing. They were to be seen marching in Selma, running health and Head Start programs for migrant workers, brandishing placards in front of chancery buildings. *Life* magazine featured "Sister J" (Jacqueline Grennan, SL), the intrepid, self-possessed president of Webster Groves College (St. Louis, Mo.). The bright splashes of Corita Kent's art linked faith with homely realities (the Virgin Mary and a ripe tomato, for instance), delighting—and horrifying—many. Newspapers and popular magazines spoke of the "new nuns." Long one of the most dependable agents in upholding and transmitting the Catholic tradition in both spirit and practice, the sisters now seemed inventive crafters of the new.

The fact is, however, that the process of change in American women's communities had begun well before Vatican II. Two initiatives in particular—one conceived by the women themselves, the other by the Vatican—were critical in the transformation of American sisters. Both prompted change and both established networks later to prove invaluable for the organization of planned change.

The first of these, the Sister Formation Movement, was, without question, the single most critical ground for the radical transformative process following Vatican II. First, it converted American sisters into the most highly educated group of nuns in the church and placed them among the most highly educated women in the United States. Second, it became the vehicle for the transmission of common ideas and a common language about change in religious life. Third, it effected the first mass shift in the worldview of American sisters.

The movement originated in the honest admission that, although they were dedicated and worked very hard, the sisters who staffed American Catholic schools lacked adequate intellectual preparation for their task. In the forties a doctoral dissertation on the state of professional preparation among teaching sisters attracted the attention of several sister academics.[1] That study was followed by a troubling presentation, "The Education of Our Young Religious Sisters,"[2] at the annual National Catholic Education Association (NCEA) meeting in 1949. In 1952 an NCEA survey of American teaching sisters confirmed that their professional preparation did, indeed, show grave lacks. By 1953 the Sister Formation Conference (SFC)[3] had been established as a committee of the Association. Under the energetic leadership of Mary Emil Penet, IHM, the SFC launched a national, broadly supported movement enlisting major superiors, college presidents and faculty, formation directors, and the newer members of women's communities in the herculean effort to enable sisters to complete baccalaureate degrees before they began teaching. Community heads began to assign increased numbers of their members to full-time college study, delaying the entrance of new members into the classroom, withdrawing others who were already teaching for sabbaticals. Parish priests and bishops protested. They wanted their schools staffed. But the heads held firmly to their course anchored by the knowledge that their colleagues in other communities were under the same pressure. It did not hurt that Vatican officials looked favorably on these early efforts of the American women and that a staff member of the Congregation for Religious (the Vatican department in charge of matters related to religious orders around the world) regularly taught in the programs for formation directors and community superiors.

A few institutions known as Sister Formation colleges with inter-community faculties and student bodies were founded. Since most of the sisters attended Catholic colleges operated by their orders, however, the SFC sought general curricular reform to incorporate both theological and social-behavioral fields. With Ford Foundation funding, the SFC convened the landmark Everett Conference in 1956, a summer-long gathering of sister PhD's, to draft a model undergraduate curriculum for the sisters. Of great significance in the long run, the SFC advocated the integration of spiritual, intellectual, and professional disciplines in the initiation programs for newer members, thereby eroding long-espoused distinctions between the "sacred" and the "worldly." SFC leaders continually urged that communities send many more sisters for masters' and doctoral degrees to staff the faculties needed to educate the younger members. Thus, key groups in religious communities, including congregational officers, were being exposed to current thought in both ecclesial and social spheres.

Sister Formation Summer Institutes, which drew impressive numbers from all over the United States, targeted two groups, the formation directors and the superiors of local houses. The institutes were a novel feature of American religious life for women: they introduced, for the first time in history, systematically planned training for the women who were in charge of socializing new members and for those who directed the day-to-day existence of sisters. Suddenly they had opportunities for theological updating and for exposure to current trends in fields ranging from liturgical and scriptural renewal to the insights of psychology and sociology about structures of religious life. The faculties of the institutes were scholars from Europe as well as this country; not only theologians but sociologists and psychologists appeared on the rosters. Back home the women began referring to a common set of ideas and actors—Father (Elio) Gambari's exciting new ideas about the church, Father (Joseph) Fichter's blunt warnings about the harmful effects of authority used dictatorially, Sister Emil's unshakable belief in the limitless potential of sisters if educated as "Renaissance women." [4] One sister recalls feeling exhilarated as she listened to her formation director relaying grand ideas about a commitment to peoples and comforting ones about the legitimacy of having close friends.

For the women, who played key institutional roles in their own communities, the institutes were also unprecedented experiences of close exchange with peers in other groups. Critically, both the institutes and regular regional meetings of formation personnel and major superiors fostered cooperative action and in many cases lasting bonds of personal respect and affection. Women whose previous experience of religious life was confined within the perimeters of their own communities began to compare notes and share successes and frustrations. Mary Daniel Turner tells of a letter that circulated round robin fashion among a group of Sister Formation members; as it came to each, she would add news about things she was trying out in her program and about herself. Some of the women who labored side by side in the leadership of the LCWR through the difficult post-Vatican years of change and conflict first met and pioneered together in the Sister Formation Conference—women like Elizabeth (then called Thomas Aquinas) Carroll, RSM, Claudia Honsberger, IHM, Margaret Brennan, IHM, Francine Zeller, OSF, and Mary Daniel Turner, SNDdeN.

The influence of the SFC extended beyond its immediate constituency (community heads, directors of formation, newer entrants) to the sisters at large. The *Sister Formation Bulletin* began in 1954 with the stated purpose of being "a publicity medium on new things in Sister-formation."[5] It became the major vehicle for the transmission of information and ideas among sisters. Subscriptions went into large numbers of local convents: a 1956 questionnaire revealed that 85 percent of community heads recommended or prescribed the *Bulletin* for reading in all the local houses. And among the superiors of those local houses, 99.2 percent made the publication available to all sisters in the house and 75 percent used it for public reading (the reading-aloud to the entire group then customary in many communities).

The publication regularly reported an expansive array of meetings, conferences, lectures, and workshops for sisters all over the country. It carried descriptions of new initiatives in individual communities such as excerpts from updated customs books (manuals of "the way we do things"), adaptations in the daily horarium (the hour-by-hour schedule of the day issued by headquarters and followed in all the houses of a given community), and the decision of a community to add two more years to the period of orientation so the young sisters could finish college before their first assignment. It regularly published abstracts of work by prominent contemporary thinkers (for example, Leo Suenens, Karl Rahner, Bernard Häring) and original articles by sisters (who thereby acquired national prominence). Generous excerpts of Vatican statements on religious life in a sense democratized information about the latest word from Rome. Widely accessible to grassroots members of women's communities, the *Bulletin* was, without question, a major tool in the awakening of the sisters not only to new ideas but to the fact that change was stirring in their life.

Skimming through issues of the first few years of the *Bulletin*, one is struck by the repeated use of words like "new," "current," "contemporary needs of sisters," "modern times," "present-day conditions." As a body the items convey strongly the image of a movement underway (and gaining momentum) to make both the individual sister and the community relevant to and confident in the times. Even the voices of outsiders sounded the theme. A 1956 issue reported the findings of an SFC survey of students in Catholic high schools and colleges. Their message was that there are women who think they have a calling but hesitate to enter religious communities because they see the sisters as separated from and oblivious to the world, out of touch with reality, and uninformed about modern problems. Respondents thought sisters should be in contact with people, listen to radio and watch television, and read contemporary writings. "Why," said one, "can't Sisters be as modern as priests? They would attract more vocations."[6]

In short, prior to Vatican Council II the SFC had produced a cadre of educated American sisters with the knowledge and the skills to take charge of a planned change process. Equally important, it had facilitated the transmission and internalization within and among women's communities of "new" ideas, which were slowly affecting the image American nuns held of themselves and implanting in their consciousness the sense that a new day was at hand for religious life.[7] It is difficult to overemphasize the seminal importance of Sister Formation in the changing of American nuns. For many the SFC initiated a conceptual shift in theology and spirituality, in worldview, actually, that antedated the later experiential shift, and grounded still other, more radical, conceptual shifts. Not infrequently when one or the other of the authors concludes a lecture in which she speaks of the SFC, a sister from the audience will come up and say, "What you said about the Sister Formation Movement is just what I experienced in my community," "The Sister Formation Movement opened our community up to collaboration with other communities," "Because of the Sister Formation Movement our community was really ready to go when Vatican II gave the word," "Some of the most creative people at our renewal assembly after Vatican II were products of the Sister Formation Movement's insistence on educating more sister PhD's."

As American sisters were becoming aware of the shortcomings of teacher preparation, the Vatican was setting in motion another process—bringing together the heads of religious communities in national associations. The movement was launched through the First General Congress of the States of Perfection, an international gathering of the heads of religious orders convoked by Pius XII in 1950. He spoke to this Congress of his belief that in World War II human history had come to a critical point. He saw modern Western society as a spiritual wasteland crying out for redemption. If a new, organized kind of collaboration were to develop among communities (particularly the women's), the church, he felt, would have a powerful instrument for the transformation of society. James Tucek calls the 1950 Congress "a revolutionary undertaking." It aimed not only "to create a mass movement of renewal" but "to defeat the immobility which had stricken many religious [communities] which had grown stale in their outdated methods and traditions."[8]

Two years later Pius XII convened a second international gathering, this time for the heads of women's communities only. Again Pius reiterated the theme of collaboration. This time he added a plea for "aggiornamento," that is, for updating certain aspects of religious life and of community works. The sisters must, he emphasized, adapt to the demands of the times precisely so they could respond to the needs of modern peoples. In a statement with obvious ramifications for the later Sister Formation work, he urged the major superiors to show largesse in educating their sisters:

> When it is a question of education, pedagogy, care of the sick, artistic activities or others, a sister should have this assurance: "My superior is giving me the opportunity of a formation that places me on an equal footing with my secular colleagues." Give them also the possibility and the means of keeping their professional knowledge up to date. Of this, too, we spoke last year. We repeat it to emphasize its importance for your sisters' peace of mind and for their work.[9]

It is said that the moving spirit behind this First World Congress of Mothers General (September 11–13, 1952) was Archbishop Arcadio Larraona.[10] A Spaniard then second in command and later head of the Congregation for Religious,[11] Larraona was a friend and confidant of Pius. He was keenly interested in religious life, particularly women's communities, and a serious student of the church's law governing religious orders. Certainly he played a central role in the Congress. In opening remarks, Larraona characterized as a "movement" the process that Pius XII had initiated with the 1950 Congress. Occasioned by the Holy Year (1950), he said, the movement began tentatively. Rome itself had no clear idea exactly where the movement should be headed, just a sense that there should be movement. Rome did not plan to force anything on religious communities, much less attempt to supplant the vision of their founders. "The movement," he said, "could be described, in a word, as a sincere effort *to keep pace with the times* [*aggiornamento;* emphasis added]." Not content with theoretical generalities about change, Larraona devoted a special session of the Congress to practical changes. He observed bluntly that custom books, with their focus on the detailed regulation of minutiae, had become "oppressive" or at least "embarrassing." He raised questions about specific areas: the archaic habits worn by many communities, the abolition of class distinctions in order to bring about "absolute equality of rights and obligations" within communities, and the use of vernacular languages (rather than Latin) for praying the Office if the change fostered spiritual development.

In the years following the Congresses of 1950 and 1952, Larraona and others in the Congregation for Religious consistently sounded the theme of renewal. When sisters expressed doubts about whether his innovations were in the spirit of their founders, he would reply, "Do not concern yourself with what your founder did in times past; consider rather what he [*sic*] would do if *today* he were alive and acting." [12] Elio Gambari spoke of "the movement for the adaptation of the religious life." From the outset, he said, "it has been clearly stated that this adjustment will embrace *everything* [emphasis added] that pertains to the religious life." He added the then revolutionary idea that the chief objective of the renewal was "to give greater value to a person as an individual. . . . No one today will any longer accept the idea of acting without awareness of what he [*sic*] is doing, merely because he has been told to act thus by authority." [13]

The Vatican did more than talk about renewal. Officials of the Congregation for Religious moved determinedly, if circumspectly (they did not want to be seen as intruding on the turf of local bishops), to promote the organization of major superiors. They initiated the convocation of national congresses in one country after another and then moved to advocate the establishment of permanent associations of heads of communities. By 1957, when Pius XII convened a Second General Congress of the States of Perfection, twenty-five national organizations had come into existence. The women and men who attended the Second Congress came not as heads of individual communities but as representatives of these conferences, among them the fledgling Conference of Major Superiors of Women of the USA.

In the United States the movement toward the organization of the leadership of religious communities got underway with the First National Congress of Religious of the USA (August 9–13, 1952). Early that year Cardinal Valerio Valeri, head of the Congregation for Religious, appointed two committees to plan the Congress. Although some events were to be held jointly, the bulk of the program would proceed in two separate tracks, one for the men, one for the women. (In fact, the Vatican sent two different lists of suggested topics to the two committees.) The National Sisters Committee consisted of seven nuns from six different communities. All but one, Sister Madeleva Wolff, CSC, were heads of religious communities though Wolff had by then achieved national prominence not only as a poet but also as one of the influential leaders of the Sister Formation Movement. Now the theme of renewal was struck with explicit reference to the American scene. Writing to Mother Gerald Barry, OP, whom the Congregation for Religious had named chair of the committee, Edward Heston, CSC, noted that the proposed United States congress would have the same objective as the First General Congress of 1950, that is, enabling religious communities "to meet the difficulties of these present times without in any way sacrificing any of the basic principles of the religious life." He added words that to American nuns then held not only praise but mandate:

> On this point the [Congregation] has high hopes regarding what it can expect from the religious of the United

States. They feel that, with our spirit of initiative and our greater freedom in making experiments, we are in a position to prove to other countries that modern adaptations can be made on certain aspects of the religious life without sacrificing anything essential.[14]

Correspondence between Heston and the planning committee indicates that the Vatican had two main objectives: to push religious communities toward the adaptation of both internal practice and external works to the exigencies of the modern world and to convince the leadership that collaboration among these communities was indispensable to apostolic (that is, ministerial) effectiveness. In fact, statements from the Congregation for Religious consistently linked *adaptation* and *organization* (for collaboration). "For the first time," wrote Barry to the heads of all communities, "the Sacred Congregation of [*sic*] Religious is inviting members of Religious Orders in this country to work and reflect together and to inquire directly into their problems and needs" in the light of "present day conditions."[15] Larraona himself attended the First National Congress, delivering both opening and closing addresses. He spoke of the "forward-looking movement" inaugurated by the 1950 General Congress and of the "generous and enlightened spirit of keeping pace with the times." "We must live in our times and according to the needs of our times," he declared.[16] It was understood, of course, that the movement for change would leave the "essentials" of religious life intact.

Months after the National Congress, Heston wrote to the members of the planning committee. Larraona, he said, wanted the committee to remain in place as a kind of permanent central organ to influence communities and cooperate "in the work of adapting certain aspects of the religious life to the needs of modern times."[17] It might also serve as a "front" for occasional gatherings of the chief officers of communities in the United States. Not much happened though. The committee met once, in April, 1954, and decided to undertake no new projects but to meet periodically to discuss issues of concern to the church.

Then, in the spring of 1956, came a new request from the Vatican: would the National Sisters Committee consider the merits of a national conference of religious and promote the idea among their women colleagues?[18] The committee met, thought about it, and concluded that no such organization was needed in the United States. A number of organizations already existed to promote the interests of education and health care such as the NCEA, the Catholic Hospital Association, and the National Catholic Welfare Conference (the bishops' conference). But the Vatican persisted; so the women agreed that if "the Holy Father" thought such conferences were necessary, the women superiors of the United States would surely cooperate.

Within six months, from April to November of 1956, these seven women drafted statutes, obtained preliminary Vatican approval for them, negotiated with a parallel committee of men superiors, and convoked a national gathering of the heads of women's communities. In the course of their work they reached the decision that the women superiors would be better served by forming their own organization rather than joining the men in a single conference. And, although the Vatican had presumed there would be a single conference in each country (in most instances that is the norm), they accepted the women's reasoning that the divergent interests and problems of sisters and of the clergy as well as the disproportionate ratio of women to men made separate conferences preferable.

On November 24, 1956, over 235 heads of American women's communities met in Chicago to decide whether they would in fact vote to band into a national conference.[19] The assembly received the recommendations of the organizing committee, reviewed the proposed statutes, and proceeded to the business at hand: deciding whether to found a conference. The ambivalence the organizing committee had experienced earlier now resurfaced in their colleagues. They were not convinced that a conference was needed and the attendant costs warranted. On the other hand, American sisters of the 1950s were not inclined to refuse Rome. From the floor came a compromise proposal that they experiment with a conference for one year before a decisive vote. And also from the floor[20] came the argument that silenced all objections: "Rome wishes it, and . . . as obedient children of the church, there should be no hesitancy in forming it." The vote was unanimous.

Thus was born the Conference of Major Superiors of Women of the USA (CMSW), today called the Leadership Conference of Women Religious of the USA (LCWR).[21] It is an association of the major officers of Roman Catholic women's communities in the United States of America. Eligibility for membership, then, is tied to formal leadership roles in the individual communities. Officially recognized and sanctioned, it has legal status as a church body and is, according to church law, accountable to Vatican authorities. As the one organization in the United States in which women come together precisely out of their roles as leaders of individual religious communities, it links those communities into a national network.

The thirty-four years of LCWR's history coincide with a period of deliberately pursued change in women's religious communities. While the story of LCWR is the story of a relatively small group of women (those in community leadership positions), the culture of the Conference is revelatory of the culture of American sisters in general. Its agendas arise from the movement of religious communities. The Conference mirrors in its history the searching of American sisters to define themselves and their meanings. Indeed, the Conference has played a critical role in that defining, and often played as critical a role in seeking the language to frame the questions and collecting the experience from which pieces of answers may be constructed. In the records of the LCWR, one can trace major patterns in the transformation of American sisters—in their conceptions of identity, in their descriptions of the way of life they choose, and, critically, in their ways of knowing and constructing those images and concepts.

Some of the lines of change can be inferred from a study of the mission of the Conference, its organizational structures, and the formulation of its relations with church authority. The basic elements of the picture are contained in two moments of the story: the founding in 1956 and the organizational restructuring in 1968–71.

The evolution of the LCWR's perception of its own mission is an important index of a changing self-definition. In just over three decades since its founding the Conference has moved to appropriate its own power to act on the world outside it. Even the original genius behind its founding, however, reveals the intuition that people acting in concert can exert an impact that exceeds the cumulative effect of independent agents. Pius XII's insistence on the organization of national conferences arose from his preoccupation with the ills of modern society. He was convinced that sisters could be a powerful force for the healing of the world if they shed the accretions that had left them an anomaly in current times. He was equally convinced that if religious communities were to succeed in updating customs and adapting their works to the needs of modern peoples, they would have to collaborate in an organized manner. Bernard E. Ransing, CSC, of the Congregation for Religious frequently struck this theme: "Isolation and isolated efforts are things of the past. The sharing of ideas, mutual assistance, and concerted effort are the order of the day." This trend was evident in all spheres of life since World War II and "the Church cannot be, and is not, a stranger to it." National conferences of heads of orders had been established "to implement this movement toward union and cooperation."[22] As the fledgling LCWR began to organize, Cardinal Valeri reminded the women that much could be achieved through "close contact and common endeavor."[23]

In its beginnings the LCWR contented itself with a highly circumscribed area of activity corresponding to the similarly circumscribed sphere then considered appropriate for sisters. Its primary purpose was, the 1956 statutes noted, "the promotion of the spiritual welfare" of American sisters and "an ever-increasing efficacy in their apostolate." Actually, the first of these dominated. Since other organizations already tended to issues connected with institutional works, the organizing committee felt that the American major superiors didn't need to devote much energy to the field of ministry. They were in the enviable position of being able to concentrate on "problems of a strictly religious nature such as affect superiors and their subjects in the observance of the religious life, especially in the light of modern demands and conditions."[24] According to the statutes, the Conference was also to foster cooperation with all religious, priests, bishops, and Catholic associations and represent the concerns of American sisters to authorities in the church. With important exceptions, these first statutes closely followed the statutes of the Canadian Religious Conference, which already had Vatican approval. And before presenting the statutes to the American major superiors as a body, the organizers had taken care to ask the Vatican to review the draft and signal its concurrence.[25]

In its first decade the Conference generally confined its activities to the service of its immediate constituency. Early program themes were the "revitalization" of religious life, "religious government," and "holiness in the apostolate according to the mind of the Holy See." And the first national studies focused on the health of sisters, the inadequacy of their salaries, and the decrease in new recruits.

As Vatican II drew to a close, the LCWR undertook larger initiatives albeit still focusing on internal church spheres.

Grasping what seemed a historical opportunity to reconfigure their life in the framework of the times, the leadership of women's communities determined to play an active role in mapping the directions of anticipated change. Through a massive population study, the Sisters' Survey (1966–68), the Conference developed a data pool on the institutional resources of women's religious communities and national and community profiles of the beliefs and values of individual American sisters. The programs of the 1965–69 annual Assemblies introduced members to new theological concepts and offered models of processes to facilitate institutional renewal. Concurrently (1965–68), the Conference involved its members in a detailed examination and critique of the legal code governing religious life. From this work came a monograph, *Proposed Norms for Consideration in the Revision of Canon Law* (Washington, D.C.: CMSW, 1968), containing principles to guide revision and model canons expressing their views on what the law for religious should include.[26] Vatican Council II touched more than the projects of the Conference. It was also affecting the self-perception of the group and the definition of its purpose. Just twelve years after the founding of the Conference, its members undertook a thoroughgoing self-study out of which came new statutes (now called "bylaws") and a new title, the Leadership Conference of Women Religious. The reorganization was more than cosmetic.

Interestingly, it originated in the Sisters' Survey, the Conference's first major national initiative to assist communities in planning for change. In 1967, as the first reports of Survey findings were being disseminated, the Research Committee directing the project recommended that the Conference examine itself in the light of Council principles. The recommendation reflected the clear finding of the Survey that American sisters in general wanted participation in decision-making. If so, it behooved the leadership to examine their own organizational behavior.[27]

In 1969 the National Executive Committee hired the management firm of Booz, Allen, Hamilton for a substantive self-study. Questionnaires were sent to all members and personal interviews conducted with over one hundred of them. On the basis of its findings, the firm drafted a set of proposed bylaws, presented to the membership at a special Assembly in 1970. Paragraph by paragraph, the Assembly debated statements of purpose and goals, measures to extend to all members the right to participate in choosing Conference officers, reconfiguration of regions, and membership eligibility. The bylaws were redrafted and once more critiqued by the members. The document ultimately adopted by the Assembly of 1971 was thus the offspring of the entire organization. The leadership had not informed or consulted Congregation for Religious officials either before or during the restructuring. The omission was not, recalls Angelita Myerscough, ASC, premeditated. "It was a process by which we took into our own hands the initiative to revise the pattern by which we were operating. . . . Perhaps we should have consulted them but at the time it didn't occur to me and I doubt if it occurred to anyone. We knew in the final analysis that the Congregation [for Religious] would have the final say on approving or not approving."[28]

The 1971 bylaws of the LCWR shifted the focus from matters concerning "superiors and their subjects" to the "development of creative and responsive leadership" and to "those forms of service consonant with the evolving Gospel mission of women religious in the world through the Church."[29] The objectives of the Conference were to support the "leadership service" of the members not simply within their communities but in the church and, through the church, in the world. The scope of collaboration was enlarged to include all "groups concerned with the needs of contemporary society." In a clear extension of mission, the new statement of purpose asserted the intent of the Conference to utilize its potential "for effecting constructive attitudinal and structural changes."

The new bylaws also reflected the women's recognition that both the world and the mission of women religious are "evolving." By implication, the specific programs of the Conference would emerge as changing conditions in church and world demanded. In contrast to their founding sisters, the women who framed these bylaws perceived themselves to be actors whose stage was the whole world. As designated leaders of their communities in a church whose mission excluded no human concern, they considered themselves responsible for bringing their collective power to bear on the needs of contemporary humanity. Their power would play a part not simply in filling those needs but in shaping church and society. They did not see this end as inappropriate to their identity as members of religious institutes. On the contrary, the very Gospel in which their identity was rooted required action of them.

With its new bylaws, the Conference, now LCWR, opted for presence and influence in an expanded field. By the end of the sixties numbers of American sisters, like many of their compatriots, had joined the movements reshaping society—the civil rights movement, the drive for incorporation of minorities into formerly white male enclaves (college faculties and student bodies, for example), the renascent women's rights struggles, and the new consciousness of poor nations. Fired up in part by the Council's document *The Church in the Modern World*, by the statement of the first post-Vatican II synod of bishops, *Justice in the World*, and by Paul VI's ringing challenge, "How then will the cry of the poor find an echo in your lives?" in his 1971 exhortation to religious, *Evangelica Testificatio* (no. 18), American sisters found themselves increasingly driven to incorporate "action on behalf of justice and participation in the transformation of the world"[30] into their formulations of religious identity. All these currents left their mark on the women of the LCWR, affecting their organizational identity and mission. Though maintaining their attention to religious life, they recast this priority into a focus on "the existential role of women religious in a constantly evolving world" (Bylaws of the Leadership Conference of Women Religious, Article II, section 1, A/LCWR). The earlier intent to collaborate with Catholic associations broadened to include "groups concerned with the needs of contemporary society" and now, in addition, the members undertook "to exercise the potential of the Conference for effecting constructive attitudinal and structural changes" (Bylaws, Article II, section 3).

The striking redirection of the conference's mission did not take place without struggle. As the women worked on statements of purpose and objective, some members proposed that the word "spiritual" be inserted to modify "leadership." They were uneasy about trends that seemed to them to spell the "secularization" of American sisters. Religious life, they insisted, was primarily concerned with things of the spirit and not of the world. And it followed, then, that the major preoccupation of the leaders of religious communities should be the spiritual as opposed to the worldly (the political or social). But other members disagreed.[31] In the end the Assembly defeated an amendment to add the modifier.

The shift in self-definition reflected in the 1971 mission statement was not the only sign that a transformation was underway. Another was the total overhauling of organizational structures to expand participation and access.

In the organization configured by the statutes, power was concentrated in the hands of a very small group, the National Executive Committee. The membership exercised little voice except in electing the three officers of their region. The eighteen regional officers constituted the National Executive Committee, which, in turn, elected the three Conference officers (National Chairman, Vice Chairman, and Secretary-Treasurer). This body made the few corporate decisions required by the limited functions of the Conference. From the Committee came the themes for each year's programming in and by the six regions. The bylaws adopted in the reorganization process, on the other hand, opened the way for continuing inclusion of the members in organizational processes.

Indeed, the major reason cited for a review of the organization's statutes in 1967 was the growing desire of members to participate more actively in the decision-making processes of the Conference. The Sisters' Survey demonstrated that American sisters in general shared that desire. The LCWR itself had, in 1965, unanimously adopted a resolution asking church officials for a voice in matters affecting their lives and for the appointment of sisters to the various commissions that would implement Vatican II. And there were rumblings of dissatisfaction in the Conference about the lack of participation in selection of national officers and formulation of organizational directions.

Restructuring the organization in the late sixties extended to the entire membership a vote in the election of national officers. An annual membership gathering called the National Assembly became a key element of structure. Redefined as "the fundamental legislative body" of the Conference, the Assembly was charged with determining its "policies and directives" and receiving and approving the report of the president (Bylaws, Article IV, section 1).

Even before the bylaws were completed, the Conference implemented universal suffrage in the election of Conference officers. And earlier still, the National Executive Committee, acting on recommendations of the Booz, Allen, Hamilton report, appointed a committee to design a resolution process through which members could bring their concerns to the National Assembly in the form of proposals for stands and actions to be voted on by the membership. At the 1969 Assembly the members acted, for the first time, on resolutions that had worked their way through a process originating in regions or committees and culminating in debate and voting by the members gathered in Assembly. The content of the resolutions embraced a range of concerns from loyalty to Paul VI as the Vicar of Christ to support of the embattled community of the Immaculate Heart sisters of Los Angeles (some of whose practices put them in conflict with church authorities). Over the years the organization has continued tinkering with the resolution process, seeking a combination of steps to ensure universal access, the right of members to request the Assembly's response to specific concerns, and sufficient information and time to protect members from a sense of pressure to conform.

Especially since the early seventies, the LCWR has involved the members in carrying out the programs and activities of the organization. In 1971–72 the National Board appointed a committee on committees to design a system of permanent committees for the work of the Conference. In its deliberations the committee explicitly cited involvement of the members as a means of tapping their creativity and experience and developing their leadership capacities. The criteria for membership in committees included the ability to work collaboratively as well as initiative and creativity. For over two decades the organization has used members to design the annual Assembly and to execute specific programs such as projects on religious life, the spiritual experience of women, and peace and disarmament. The organization also calls on members to represent it on the boards of other organizations and at religious and civic events.

To engender participation the Conference gradually strengthened the networking of members with one another and the creation of processes to share experience and knowledge, to understand one another's viewpoints, and to learn together. Indeed, the LCWR bylaws lists among its objectives "to provide mutual support to one another" (Bylaws, Article II, section 3). Since 1974, for example, Assembly planning committees have explicitly adverted to the process design of the gatherings, devoting at least as much attention to the manner of participant interaction as to the content of major addresses and workshops. In one Assembly after another, a mix of input, conversation in small and intermediate groups, and dialogue in the total body seeks to capitalize on relationships among members as a key vehicle for probing the meaning of ideas and their implications for personal and collective experience.

The general circulation of information was also improved to widen access. Beginning in 1971 the first popularly elected president, Angelita Myerscough, introduced the annual president's report (now called the Conference Report) chronicling the year's activities and presenting the budget and audit reports. An evaluation form solicits individual member concurrence with or reservations about Conference activities and the decisions of the leadership. Evaluation forms for each Assembly also gather membership input not only on the event just completed but also on directions for the next year's meeting. Since 1974 one or more sessions of the National Assembly are dedicated to the communication and discussion of sensitive information (for example, the officers' efforts to assist in the resolution of conflicts with Vatican authorities). On several occasions the National Board decided to transmit such information orally to the members through the regional chairpersons (who represent the regions on the governing body) so that the internal constituency would be aware of critical issues and informed about the leadership's interventions. A monthly newsletter communicates the ordinary activities of the officers, the national office, and various task forces.

If the changes in mission and structure shed light on movements among American sisters, so does the reorientation of institutional relations between the Conference and church authority. The first statutes asserted that the Conference "depends immediately" on the Congregation for Religious. The women made explicit their resolve to show "perfect allegiance" to the hierarchy in the United States and said they would "submit" to diocesan authorities when appropriate.[32]

Before presenting the statutes to the founding convocation for review, the organizing committee had made sure of the *nihil obstat*[33] of Cardinal Valeri. Almost immediately they had asked for the appointment of Bernard Ransing, then a staff member at the Congregation for Religious, as their ecclesiastical advisor.

Reorganization debates and the resulting purpose statement in the new bylaws left no doubt that the women of the reorganization also understood themselves as ecclesial persons, intending the Conference to serve the mission of the church to the world. They understood that church, however, less as institution than as People of God in mission. The highly juridical phrasing of the Conference's relation to the church was largely absent from the draft of the bylaws adopted by the 1971 National Assembly. Like the issue of "spiritual leadership" cited earlier, this topic became a source of controversy in the reorganization process. Some members saw the omission of the language of immediate "dependence" on the Congregation for Religious as a sign of diminished allegiance to the church and, along with the first issue, as evidence of a tendency to "secularize" religious life.

The new bylaws and the new name were presented to the Congregation for Religious for approval in October, 1971, after the Assembly had adopted them. Subsequent dialogue among the officers of the organization, the National Board, and the Congregation for Religious[34] led to the addition of language acknowledging a "due regard for the authority of the Holy See and of the bishops" and noting that the Conference "relates directly" to the Congregation. A provision requiring approval by the Holy See of future amendments to the bylaws was also added. Further, the bylaws stipulated that the Conference inform the Apostolic Delegate of "its more important activities."[35] Where the CMSW statutes had spoken of "dependence," the LCWR bylaws cited "relationship." Vatican approval of the bylaws came in 1972.

Approval of the change of name was a different story. Officials of the Congregation as well as the Vatican's ambassador to the United States voiced strong objections to the word "leadership." It smacked of arrogance, suggesting that Americans were the leaders of religious communities of women; it was reminiscent of Fascist titles like "Il Duce" and "der Fuhrer"; it was secular. Asked what she thought was the reason for the struggle over the change in name, Ann Virginia Bowling, IHM, answered, "The word 'leadership.'" She told of a meeting between Thomas Aquinas (Elizabeth) Carroll, RSM, the Conference president, and the Vatican ambassador. "They both had dictionaries and they both looked up the word 'leader' and the word 'leadership.' To my recollection," she continued, "Rome never questioned shedding the old name." But "we should not consider ourselves leaders."[36] A former president speculated that church authorities couldn't stomach connecting women with leadership. Finally, in 1974, after lengthy discussions, the Vatican acceded on condition that the title be followed by the sentence, "This title is to be interpreted as: the Conference of Leaders of Congregations of Women Religious of the United States of America." Recalled Bowling, "Several bishops wrote back what a ridiculous footnote this was; anybody would know [what the title meant]." The struggle over the name proved to be a harbinger of Vatican response to American initiatives.

The remaining chapters of this book study the process of reidentification, each standing at a different vantage point to examine the movement. Chapter Two examines the transformation of definitions of religious life. The most theoretical of the chapters, it shows the unraveling of faith concepts like "the religious" and "the world" as new experiences challenged the premises on which the meaning of religious life had hinged. It lays out the equally important unraveling of learning processes. Chapter Three traces the impact of American culture on the sisters and the resulting struggles to reconcile American belonging and religious commitment into one identity. In Chapter Four we explore the sisters' gradual awakening to the reality of gender as an element of personal and corporate identity and their even more gradual (and ambivalent) confronting of the structural questions that occur to awakened women. Chapter Five speaks of their development as moral agents, focusing on how the sisters are repositioning themselves in relation to responsibility and, thus—inevitably—to authority. And the final chapter examines the peculiar interlacing of change with conflict that has characterized the journey of American nuns since the mid-sixties. The five rubrics are one way of telescoping what is, without doubt, a complex social passage achieved in a remarkably brief time. The neatness of distinctions suggested by this outline is, of course, belied by the often desultory course of life. The five themes and the experiences connected with each intercross at numerous junctures. We have indicated some of the linkages; readers will see others.

The language of self-image is a telling index of the speaker's perceptions of who she is and what universe she inhabits. Two images, buried in the annals of the LCWR, wonderfully capture the passages of American sisters. In 1957 the first national "chairman" of the CMSW, Mother Alcuin McCarthy, OSF, attended the Second General Congress of the States of Perfection in Rome as an official representative of the new conference. The first woman ever to stand in an international forum as the spokesperson of American sisters united for purposes yet to unfold, she concluded her report with a description of the women back home:

> We [American sisters] devote ourselves to the traditional works of education of youth and the care of the sick. . . . We walk with firm and steady steps behind our leaders—the illustrious hierarchy of our country, our beloved Apostolic

Delegate, the reverend members of the Sacred Congregation for the Affairs of Religious, and our great and glorious present Holy Father. To all we pledge our loyalty and filial devotion.[37]

Fourteen years later the Conference, already caught up in the refashioning of religious life, neared the Assembly, which would approve new structures and a new name, chosen by the women. The first president elected by universal suffrage, Angelita Myerscough, addressed the first formal report to her peers. To them she spoke of her hopes:

I believe that we can become committed to greater service not only to our own membership but to women religious throughout the country, to our fellow citizens, and especially to the poor. CMSW can become a powerful force for good in the United States and in the world. Ours is the power of dedicated Christian womanhood, anxious to love and to serve and to penetrate the world with the message of the Gospel.[38]

Chapter Two / On the Way to a Different Place

ONE THING SEEMS STABLE and certain: the fact of change. Those whose adulthood lies within the past fifty years can assert this, not on the authority of theorists of social change but on their own authority. They have known massive change, benefiting and suffering from it whether or not they have chosen to advance it. Change has brought about a kind of universal dislocation—and not simply in terms of physical rupture with familiar settings and ways. Concepts have altered, worldviews have disintegrated, wisps of new paradigms float inconclusively in the air. A kind of knowledge-quake is in process, unmooring familiar guideposts. No one is quite sure what the new mind order, the new world order will be. And many, witnessing the shakiness of human formulations long touted as the truth, resist any construction suggesting dogmatism in either the content or the process of knowledge.

Nowhere, we suggest, is this more clearly evident than among American sisters. Their place in both church and world has been jarred loose, their communities shaken up. Sisters appear in worldly dress, occupy houses among ordinary folks, work in secular agencies, and participate in grassroots movements. The visible modifications also signal a substantive alteration in the way American sisters know and think about religious life. That is, a transformation has occurred in both the *content* of the construct "religious life" and the *epistemological processes* by which sisters know their life and its meaning. Traditional formulations of religious life have been revised, even totally recast. The more pivotal change, however, has occurred in the processes sisters have been developing to discover and appropriate knowledge. Emphasizing both historicity and experience, the processes used to apprehend reality have empowered sisters to claim the responsibility for determining their own identity and the meaning of religious life instead of simply receiving it from external authority. This kind of change virtually assures the continuation of the movement of change that will impact religious life in ways now only dimly envisioned.

Having a Place, Enclosed and Secure

It is critical to understand that the transformation of knowing and knowledge is not simply one among a host of changes. Nor is it an exercise in the spinning of pure theory. For sisters, acquiring knowledge about religious life, consciously (and self-consciously) thinking about and understanding religious life, has traditionally been a central preoccupation. The proper study of nunkind was nuns. The theory of religious life has always been a formal field of study for the women who opt for that life. And study of the theory of religious life is no mere mental exercise; it provides, rather, a total worldview. It incorporates concepts of God and of ultimacy, of the church and its mission, of humankind and human endeavor, of the good society, of personal identity and moral choice, of good and evil, and it tries to account for the interrelation of all these.

Women who enter religious communities devote one or two years exclusively to formation (that is, formal socialization into religious life and the specific community they have joined). Until well into the sixties the central component of initial formation was the study of theological and legal (principally the latter) definitions of religious life and its obligations as well as the rules and "customs" ("the way we do things") of the community. The body of knowledge to which new members were introduced was *received* knowledge, often formulaic in structure. Thus, it was not unusual for the novices to memorize assigned portions of the *Catechism of the Religious Profession*, a compendium of questions and answers whose title page bore the phrase "translated from the French and revised in conformity with the new code of canon law."[1] The catechism proceeded, topic by topic, to pose questions like "What is a vow?" "How do the vows of religion enable us to surmount the most serious obstacles to the love of God?" "What is perfection?" "What are the obligations of a Superior towards his [sic] inferiors in regard to poverty?" "Is a permission given by a Superior valid under his successor?" "What obligation does a Religious assume by the vow of obedience?" "Why is the vow of obedience the most excellent of the vows of religion?" Very succinct answers consisted of definitions, norms, lists of obligations, and distinctions among degrees of culpability—all asserted as *fact*. The questions had been formulated by others (chiefly ordained males) and were designed to instruct the neophytes on topics the authors considered important. The answers were standard and indisputable, basically distillations of the church's law governing religious life.

Experience got short shrift as a source of knowledge about religious life and how it should be lived. That experience could be the basis for revising theory was an unthinkable notion within the reigning worldview. Existing theory was there before new members arrived and would remain when they moved on. It was applied deductively to concrete cases and everyday problems. For example, what should a sister do if it was time for community prayer and a student wanted to talk to her? Or again, if a good friend who knew a sister before she entered the order (as distinct from one who met her in her capacity as "Sister," the sixth-grade teacher) gave her a gift, could she retain it for personal use or did it, by virtue of the vow of poverty, automatically belong to the community?

Studying and thinking about religious life did not cease when the women completed their formation. It continued throughout their lives. Their rule obliged sisters to spend some time every day on "spiritual" reading from books dealing with religious life and growth in "the spiritual life." Yearly they made retreats, extended periods of total silence during which the retreat master, always a priest, preached on each of the vows, on sundry virtues, on self-discipline and penance, on one's relationship with God, on spiritual growth, and on charity toward and service to fellow human beings. Daily meditation and examinations of conscience demanded that sisters consciously focus on the congruence between their choices and the norms of religious life. From their first days in the community, an essential part of their living was the deliberate pursuit of knowledge pertaining to the theory of religious life. That theory consciously grounded who they perceived themselves to be, how they understood their commitment, what choices they made, and what actions they believed appropriate.

The single most important idea, the linchpin, of the worldview from which sisters derived their meaning was that the sacred and the secular were separate and distinct realities. The sacred was the domain of the perfect and changeless; the secular, of change and the ephemeral. The church and the spiritual life belonged to the first ("the City of God"); the world and human endeavor belonged to the second ("the City of Man"). The first was of the "supernatural" order; the second, of the "natural." Religious life lay wholly in the realm of the sacred.

Beginning in 1917 when church law governing religious life was codified,[2] women joining active communities of sisters understood they were called to a privileged state in the church. Leaving the world, freely renouncing their "worldly" name, putting on "religious" garb, they entered the "state of perfection." Ordinary Christians were obliged to be good and to observe the commandments. Sisters took upon themselves the "higher" obligations of the evangelical counsels (poverty, celibacy, and obedience) and of constant striving for holiness. By publicly professing the three vows, they declared their intention of belonging only to God and dedicating every single moment of their lives to loving and serving God. Entering religious life meant irrevocably disavowing the world.

This profession elevated them above the laity (though leaving them below the clergy and hierarchy). As consecrated persons they were the visible, public witnesses of the kingdom of God, a kingdom not of this world. The spiritual life, that is, prayer, self-abnegation, silence, recollection, and the practice of the vows, was to be their sole preoccupation. "Religious life," in short, was about personal holiness. The opening sentence of the rule of one community read, "The primary end of the Institute of the Sisters of Divine Providence is the sanctification (that is, the attaining of holiness) of its members by the practice of the three vows of Poverty, Chastity, and Obedience, and the observance of these Constitutions." (It is not unusual, when one or the other author uses this sentence to exemplify a point in a lecture, for her to find the audience chanting the words along with her as sisters delightedly discover that a formula they thought unique was ubiquitous.)

Sisters in active communities engaged in works of mercy, teaching, nursing, caring for orphans, and feeding the poor. But, as religious, sisters were enjoined to be concerned less with the physical needs of those they served and more with uniting their souls with God and securing their eternal happiness. However praiseworthy, works undertaken to serve the neighbor were defined as secondary, distinct and separate from sisters' religious identity. (The rule cited above went on to say, "The secondary end is the Christian education and instruction of children and young ladies and the care of the sick." Similar sentences appeared in all community rules.) As a consequence, participation in general church life even at the parish level was not encouraged. Involvement in the social, cultural, and political arenas was simply unthinkable. At its most innocent, "the world" distracted sisters from their fundamental commitment, the pursuit of holiness; at its worst, it was a temptation to sin. Thus, in so-called "apostolic" communities involved in the active works of education, health care, and social services, a curious split existed between "religious life" and "apostolic works." The split rested on the sacred/secular dichotomy. Were the two ever in conflict, there was no question but that "religious life" would receive priority.[3]

This antisecular and ahistorical orientation inevitably produced in many religious a mindset that understood "religious life" to be a real thing. It had an existence in its own right independent of and prior to actual religious communities and their living, breathing members. An enduring "essence," untouched by the passage of time, it was impervious to alterations in human arrangements. Canonical definitions, legislated by church authorities, gave "religious life" its existence, its legitimacy, and its value. In addition, church law provided reliable norms in the light of which experience was to be constructed and tested. Fidelity to these norms guaranteed the authenticity of one's life. One might chafe at restrictions, find them incomprehensible, even rebel against them. Ordinarily, however, such attitudes would have been judged a problem of the rebel (who was said to "lack a vocation"), or of the community (which had grown lax), or of temptations against one's vocation (the work of the evil spirit). Religious life in the concrete could not be otherwise because "religious life" was not otherwise in essence.

Dislocated, but Not Lost

The formulations of Vatican Council II wrenched American sisters from the security of these firmly held faith convictions. Cast into uncharted territory they wrestled with the truth of their life—its meaning and their identity. And if a pre-Vatican worldview made certain changes unthinkable, Vatican II made them imperative. As one of the pioneers of renewal, Elizabeth

Carroll, RSM, writes, "The publication of the documents of Vatican II gave new direction to all the instincts, questions, and restlessness operating under the surface of a very uniform life. The 'Universal Call to Holiness' overturned a theology of religious life that had prevailed for 1500 years."[4]

Imaging the entire church as a single People with one single mission, the Council Fathers declared that all the baptized are called to holiness, not just a chosen few.[5] A call to the pursuit of holiness in a life consecrated wholly to God had been the special preserve of religious communities, the ground of the sisters' identity. Now *Lumen Gentium*, the Council's seminal document on the church, asserted that there is no privileged state of perfection higher than the path of ordinary goodness. Moreover, said the document, religious life is not "a kind of middle way between clerical and lay conditions of life. Rather it should be seen as a form of life to which some Christians, both clerical and lay, are called by God."[6] If religious life were not a separate state, then what of sisters? Priests, whether or not members of religious communities, could continue to use ordination as a reference point from which to maintain their sense of identity (and special calling) intact. As women, sisters cannot be clerics, so they must be those called by God from among the laity. Dislodged from a protected, clearly demarcated (and elite) "state," sisters suddenly found themselves laity.

In other words, some of the theological constructs of Vatican Council II literally dissolved, right out from under sisters, the privileged place and role they traditionally occupied. Sisters were embarked, without maps, on a road toward an unknown destination. One thing *was* clear—their new place and their new identity lay within, as a part of, humanity's uncertain journey through time. And while both *Perfectae Caritatis* and *Lumen Gentium* (Vatican II documents) gave mixed signals[7] concerning the place of sisters in the church and the world, the Council's *Gaudium et Spes* was eminently clear about the role of the church in the world. The church was *for* the world, its mission *in* the world. Such a church, alive and responsive to history's unfolding, appealed to American nuns. They began to comprehend the fact that history is an inescapable factor in answering the questions, "What is religious life?" "Who are we?" "Where are we going?"

This consciousness was not, of course, entirely new. Under the influence of the Sister Formation movement sisters had glimpsed, even if dimly, that religious life is indeed situated in history.[8] Some of the very theologians who shaped the positions of Vatican II (Karl Rahner, Yves Congar, Bernard Häring, Gregory Baum) were among those to whose thought the sisters were introduced through Sister Formation workshops and publications. The push for educational and professional mastery in the fifties had begun to erode the boundaries between the "state" of religious life and the "place" of human commerce. Experientially, too, sisters were recognizing that conditions had changed in their communities since their founding. What now characterized them had not always been so. (In one community's beginnings, for example, the sisters went alone to work in poor villages. Now they could not go downtown alone to buy a pair of shoes.) Critical meanings had been perceived and worded differently in times past. Looked at from its origins, religious life was not simply a canonically defined state of consecration separated from the world. It was, in fact, a religious response historically conditioned by the concrete events of peoples and nations and the Spirit-inspired insights of those living it. Sisters began to notice that even long-held and never-to-be-challenged philosophical and theological premises lent themselves to the purposeful sounding of experience, personal and social. Experience possessed its own authority. This new approach to learning was supported by the prominence of process philosophy, incarnational spirituality (which emphasized the immanence of God and history as the place of God's acting), and especially biblical studies.

Eventually these convictions brought forth in American sisters the capacity to trust the authority of their collectively explored experience.

Appreciating that the world might shed light on the meaning of religious commitment, sisters gradually became convinced that the world is the ground on which the church's mission is to be acted out. They began to understand that, for apostolic communities at least, immersion in the world is indispensably linked with holiness. Learning the oneness of life (personal, communal, and societal) American sisters struggled to resocialize themselves to patterns of thought, language, and behavior expressing integration with rather than separation from the world, from one another, from self—from one's moment in history. They found themselves rejecting dualisms that split the religious and apostolic dimensions of their life. For example, they abandoned the notions that "religious" holiness and presence in the world are antithetical and that "lay" life is inferior because it is lived in the world. No longer viewing their work as extraneous or secondary to their religious identity, they grasped that work and identity are inseparably related.[9] Dichotomies between being and doing ceased to make sense to many women religious. How could one distinguish dancer from dance?[10]

If entering into history and valuing human experience as a legitimate locus of "truth" transformed the relation of American sisters to the world, it revolutionized their way of knowing. This, we think, is the most far-reaching change. Sensitive to the truth that the experience of women (past and present) who have lived religious life must be taken into account in any determination of its meaning, American sisters seek congruity between their experience and church teachings. They have been learning, even if they don't use the language of epistemology, that knowledge is constructed. That is, ideas are not exact replicas of reality directly absorbed into the knowers' consciousness. Knowledge has a "man-made" history and tradition that have been handed on. It is always partial and biased. And knowledge can change. New experiences and learnings alter, even supplant, what was once accepted as true and certain. In addition, knowledge is contextual. Even basic assumptions must be illuminated by concrete historical reality and applied variously.[11] Thus, formulas reached through deductive reasoning founded on "first principles" (usually identified as fixed and absolute verities) became suspect, even untenable, to many women religious.[12]

As defined in official church statements, "religious life" has been more often than not simply a juridical construct embodying the worldviews (preferences) of jurists. The construct may or may not bear any resemblance to the life of the flesh-and-blood women forming communities in time and space. What is described in the official teachings of the Roman Catholic church as "religious life"—in its legal formulations or requirements and in its official theologies—is there because persons (all men) holding positions of authority have consciously (no doubt conscientiously) determined those constituents. Rather than describing a preexisting reality, they in fact construct it out of first principles presumed to be eternal and divinely sanctioned. And once, American sisters received these constructs as real things.

More recently, growing numbers of sisters have come to distrust ecclesiastical pronouncements concerning "religious life." Attention to experience and history has made it obvious that religious life is not a predetermined "unchanging essence." Without historical form, religious life is an abstraction, a mental fiction. Without historical groupings there is no community that authority can recognize canonically; there is no *place* to enter the life. Rather, specific religious communities with a point of origin, a story made up of events, a tradition created by generations of women making choices, and an enduring spirit are what exist. Both the history and experience of existing (as well as now defunct) communities witness to the fact that people and things change. As a result, sisters believe that history and contemporary experience not only are locuses of "truth" but also validate change.

American sisters in general see the transformation of their life as the result of a responsible good-faith effort to comply with the charge addressed to religious communities by Vatican II. The document *Perfectae Caritatis* [13] characterized the mandate to renew as a "divine call" (paragraph 25). Religious communities were exhorted to be "prompt in performing the task allotted to them in the Church today" (paragraph 25). Indeed, some apologists of the mid-sixties, including officials of the church, tied the success or failure of the church's total renewal to the course of renewal in religious communities.

The document went into some detail in delineating the scope of change being demanded:

> The manner of living, praying, and working should be suitably adapted to the physical and psychological conditions of today's religious and also, to the extent required by the nature of each community, to the needs of the apostolate, the requirements of a given culture, the social and economic circumstances anywhere, but especially in mission countries. The way in which communities are governed should also be reexamined in the light of these same standards. (paragraph 3)

A new broom, indeed! Three elements of this passage are noteworthy. The appeal to contemporaneity in form is explicit. That concrete historical experience should be normative in determining the structure of sisters' communities is equally clear and, was for the time, revolutionary in its potential for dismantling conceptual frameworks. And, finally, "the nature of each community" in effect suggests that the individual community possesses distinctive qualities that legitimately inform its living, prayer, work, and polity. Gone in one stroke was the notion that religious communities were concrete replicas of some ideal. Diverse histories, cultural and social environments, and peoples served called for diverse communities.

Having earnestly carried out the injunctions of the Council to adapt and renew every part of their lives, sisters increasingly found not credible the dicta of church officials that the changes were wrong and wrong-headed simply because they did not conform to church legislation. They were equally incredulous when told, for the same reason, that what they had wrought was not "religious life." As early as 1968, for example, the attention of both officials and sisters focused on the highly public conflict between the Immaculate Heart of Mary sisters and Cardinal James McIntyre of Los Angeles over changes legislated by their special general chapter (a legislative meeting). In April, 1968, the Vatican released a statement censuring these changes as deviations from the true nature of religious life. Officials ordered the statement circulated in all American communities of women. Sisters throughout the country went into an uproar. Debate, public and private, flourished on whether certain innovations were, as the Vatican asserted, incompatible with religious life. Wearing a habit as a symbol of consecration (and, therefore, separation from the world) and maintaining institutional works in preference to newer services in the public sphere (again, a curtailment of involvement in the world) were particularly controverted points. Since many American communities besides the IHM sisters had adopted similar provisions, discussions focused specifically on whether religious life was what church law stipulated it to be or what was developing through the experience of communities.

Sisters have become reluctant to assert that any stage religious communities have reached (or any yet to come) represents a definitive form of their life, much less *the* definitive one. What they now know is that both the life of American sisters and its theoretical underpinnings will continue to change because they happen in time. While neither ignoring nor trivializing church teachings in making choices, they nevertheless value the wisdom found in their personal and collective experiences and in the social experience of humankind. American sisters know that they, who are living religious life, must take primary responsibility for its transformation.

Although the transformation of sisters and religious life has been played out primarily in individual communities, its outline is clear in the records of the LCWR. As the formal association of the heads of these communities the Conference not only reflects the change process in its own workings, but has itself been an instrument of the process of change. Undeniably a force in the refashioning of apostolic religious life in this country, the Conference has served as a laboratory for experiments in corporate reflection, analysis, and action concerning matters of significance to American sisters. And as an official agent of collaboration with other sectors of the church (particularly those wielding institutional authority), the Conference has often found itself a party to events critical to the creation of an apostolic identity markedly different from that which prevailed before these decades. The LCWR has, in fact, played a seminal role in the reidentification of American sisters as well as in the reimaging of religious life. Three events in Conference history shed light on new ways of knowing religious life—the Sisters' Survey, the two formal studies of church law governing religious communities, and projects to construct contemporary descriptions of the life.

Relocating and Searching

The Sisters' Survey (1966–1968) was the first empirical study ever made of the collective internal life of women's communities and of the belief patterns of individual sisters in the United States. Although it proved catalytic far beyond what its creators dreamed, its origin and intent were innocuous enough. A meeting at Grailville, Ohio, in 1964—obscure but significant for the LCWR and sisters generally—provided an unusual opportunity for several American sisters. During a seminar led by Charles Davis, they gained access to an advance draft of the Vatican II document on religious life. They clustered into an informal group and talked long and hard about what the future might hold. The group was exhilarated by the possibilities this document seemed to promise. Sensing the fresh spirit at work in American communities, they believed other American sisters would respond eagerly to the decree. In fact, they knew many would welcome it as a confirmation of the renewal movement already underway in this country. Their talking led them to conceive of two ventures: publishing a book on American sisters and asking the LCWR (through Mary Luke Tobin, SL, then president of the Conference) to spearhead research to assess the resources available for planned change and the readiness of sisters for renewal. The book, *The Changing Sister*, was published in 1965.[14] Within the same year the research project was approved. The LCWR's National Executive Committee set up the Research Committee, charged with assisting women's communities in the work of renewal.[15]

Even before *Perfectae Caritatis* was released in October, 1965, then, the Research Committee was developing strategies to accomplish its mandate.[16] The committee collected institutional data from 410 different religious communities of women (for example, the number of members with graduate degrees, new entrances and departures, types of work) and information about the plans of the communities for the next ten years. The Research Committee decided it would also sample individual American sisters. The National Executive Committee recommended a total population study instead. National Executive Committee members were concerned lest a random sample result in sisters' claiming that the national profile did not apply to particular communities. Each congregation must know its own profile if the intent of the survey were to be realized, namely, to determine whether communities needed in-service training programs, updated theological study, or an immediate action plan.

With typical American pragmatism the Research Committee went to work, gathering data on 139,691 sisters (88 percent of the population surveyed).[17] To fund the study the Conference asked each community to pay one dollar per member; Research Committee members and the sociologists who compiled and analyzed the data donated their labor. For the first time in history American sisters as a group were asked to describe their beliefs about religious life and to express their views on anticipated as well as actual changes taking place in their communities. A questionnaire of some 645 items, the Sisters' Survey ranged over topics from concepts of God and of the vows to expectations for change in governance and ministry to television viewing habits. "I think of God as unchanging essence and uncaused cause," read one item. "I feel that diversity in individual men [sic], among peoples, and in many cultures helps me appreciate the meaning of the Incarnation," said another. On and on went the procession of statements. "Religious should be occupied with spiritual things leaving laymen to take care of secular matters." "If a sister shuns involvement with persons I think she betrays the purpose of her vow of chastity." "By establishing oneself in the religious state, one gives up one's independence and sets aside one's liberty." "Teaching religion is directly apostolic, other work is only indirectly so." "Catholics as a group should consider active opposition to U.S. participation in Vietnam." "Have you ever worked with the really poor?" "Would you like to see some of the sisters of your order devote their time to some of the following groups in the very near future?" (groups included drug addicts, people seeking dialogue with Communists, racial minorities, alienated youth). "Would you stand up for a sister's right in conscience to speak, write, march, demonstrate, picket, etc., when this conflicts with a higher superior's or bishop's wishes?" The very array of positions itself communicated that pluralism was possible in areas considered essential (therefore fixed) to the definition of religious life as, for example, the appropriate relation of sisters to the world and the purpose of ministry. The Survey also held out the novel idea that individual sisters might legitimately choose from among differing behaviors in both the internal life of the community and external arenas.

Simply completing the Survey was a formative experience. One sister remembers the almost physical sense of enlargement she felt when it dawned on her that there was more than one way to think about bedrock issues of faith and commitment in a religious community. Another confesses delightedly that some of the items planted ideas about things to do. "Oh," she thought, "it's okay to attend meetings of 'people other than your own religious community, the students, patients, or clients you service.'" And, "I probably should see *Nights of Cabiria* and *Wild Strawberries*" (one item asked whether respondents had seen any of a sample of foreign films). Those who trekked through the dozens of survey items could not escape awareness of current intellectual, social, and cultural trends even as they weighed alternatives and sorted out their own positions.

An especially significant facet of the survey was the use of specific theological categories as a measure of discrimination. Convinced that Vatican II was trying to generate a new understanding of the mission of the church and that "religious belief is a major determinant of (1) receptiveness to change and (2) of change,"[18] Marie Augusta Neal, SNDdeN, the research director, developed one hundred items based on what she called pre- and post-Vatican belief orientations. The items were designed to measure the dominant theological orientations of sisters and the influence of differing perspectives on change. For the content of the statements a group of religious researchers studied the documents of Vatican II in the form in which they were available in 1965–66. "To these," says Neal, "we added our understanding of the theologies of the fifties, previously analyzed, which were the background for the new directions of the Council." [19] According to Neal, "Extensive research and testing went into the construction of this measure of religious belief." It became, she notes, "the most controversial and the most discriminating variable, which accounted for the pace and direction of changes in structures of the religious congregations involved in the study." [20]

Survey findings showed that 68.2 percent of sisters shared a strong preference for post-Vatican ideals. That is, they tended to see God as acting among people in a world undergoing massive change (as opposed to God as transcendent other). They saw diverse projects directed toward social justice as places of ministry (as opposed to organized Catholic centers for the delivery of services). They believed participation in movements for the common good was the form of religious commitment (as opposed to allegiance to church authority and norms).[21] In other words, the transformation of worldview was already well underway. Findings also revealed that the heads of communities, the directors of formation, and the newer members were among the most open to change. These women—the very constituencies most directly touched by the Sister Formation movement—were in strategic positions to exercise institutional power in the coming change process.

The results of the Survey were made public in two forums. Each participating community received computer printouts of its own profile as well as the national profile; and Neal presented an interpretive report of significant findings to community heads at both the 1967 and 1968 LCWR Assemblies. Almost immediately after the Council closed, then, American sisters had graphic evidence of the immense ideological diversity already present in their midst. Since each community had access to both its own and the national profiles, sisters were informed about general patterns of thought and behavior among American sisters and of the degree to which their community did or did not reflect these patterns.

An important function of the Survey quite simply proved to be that it held up the fact of radical diversity among sisters, even on the very nature of the life they shared. For example, the item "Religious have a greater call to holiness and apostolic responsibility than do Christian laymen [sic]" elicited a response of 48.1 percent yes, 44.8 percent no. Other examples include: "I think that sisters who feel called to do so ought to be witnessing to Christ on the picket line and speaking out on controversial issues, as well as performing with professional competence among their lay peers in science labs, at conferences and on the speakers' platform" (44.1 percent yes, 31.5 percent no). "Chastity is the renunciation of all partial loves in order to embrace the perfection of love in a mystical union with Christ" (37.2 percent yes, 45.7 percent no). "The essence of religious life is the continual renunciation of one's own will" (33.9 percent yes, 54.9 percent no). "Personal sanctification comes first, then duties of the apostolate" (49.4 percent yes, 34.6 percent no). Religious life in the United States was already in flux—irrevocably.

The Sisters' Survey directly affected the initial organization of change in women's communities. Of special relevance to the response of American sisters to Vatican II was the finding that 41 percent of the communities had begun structured planning for general chapters (the name used for both the highest legislative body in a religious community and for the event of a legislative session, which occurs at regular intervals) even before the publication of *Ecclesiae Sanctae*. This Vatican document, released in 1966, set norms for the implementation of renewal in religious communities. In terms of momentum for change, perhaps the most important provision of *Ecclesiae*

Sanctae was the mandate that every community was to hold a special general chapter within three years to determine the lines of its renewal. The norms not only mandated a chapter, but directed that every sister be involved in preparations for it. This kind of universal participation was not just unusual, but revolutionary. More surprising still, religious communities were instructed to exempt no facet of their lives from scrutiny in preparing chapter agendas. Traditionally, these gatherings were the province of a very small group of elected delegates. The main function of a chapter in most communities of women was to elect the general officers of the community. Rarely was the community rule as such considered matter for scrutiny, much less for revision. *Ecclesiae Sanctae*, in effect, validated what many orders had already initiated as a part of organized planning.

The data from the Sisters' Survey were an invaluable resource for the special chapters. Not only did numberless committees pore over the national and individual profiles for evidence to bolster chapter proposals and appeal to the data in the heat of chapter debates, but the Survey was instrumental in enabling chapters to see clearly the task a community faced in living into a new image, in fact a new paradigm, of religious life. Church officials used "adaptation" and "renewal" to distinguish between two kinds of change. They intended to underscore a division between the "substance" and the "accidents" of religious life (and between that life and the world). Above all, they intended to signal that some changes were permissible and others were strictly off limits. Sisters were sensing, even if they were unable to put their hunches into language, that changes, even so-called "accidental" ones, ultimately touched the very core of their life. In actuality, adaptations in dress, schedules, and work called into question more than the practices being modified. Religious dress, schedules to guarantee regular observance, and designated appropriate works for sisters had their source in a specific worldview. The results from the Survey made only too evident that the foundations of this worldview were already eroded, more accurately, displaced. Dichotomies that had once drawn easy assent no longer held sway among a significant number of women religious. Notably, the separation between the sacred and the secular, between church and world, between consecration and mission—so long the basis of the structure of religious life—ceased to be credible to many sisters. Their experience as well as the vision of Vatican II, especially in *Gaudium et Spes, Lumen Gentium,* and the decree on *Religious Freedom,* exposed, on the one hand, the inadequacy of the classical, Western worldview of religious life and, on the other, opened up new images of being religious.

The Survey enabled American sisters to become aware, in an organized way, of their experience of and beliefs about religious life. Two other Conference projects demanded that the women examine closely and evaluate the church's law defining and regulating that life. Early in the renewal movement and once again some ten years later, the Conference carried out in-depth reviews of the law. Each time the women hoped to shape the law to be more responsive to and inclusive of the experience of American sisters.

The first study (1965–68) began even before the Council ended. In 1961, Pope John XXIII appointed a commission for the revision of the code of canon law. The commission officially began work, however, only in late 1965. Earlier that year, anticipating the commission's work, Paul Boyle, CP, president of the Canon Law Society of America, had written to Mary Luke Tobin, Conference president, asking for the women's feedback on the code. In response, the National Executive Committee set up a Canon Law Committee of Conference members to direct and coordinate the task.[22] Aided by this committee, the Conference members as a corporate body—for the first time in the history of religious communities of women—engaged in a totally women-directed evaluation of church law. Doing so put them in the novel posture of assessing official church prescriptions hitherto virtually unquestioned and constructing alternative formulations.[23]

The Canon Law Committee developed guiding principles for the critique. The basic one was "that both Pope John XXIII and Pope Paul VI . . . explicitly stated that the revision of Church law is intended to bring about the faithful application to law of the teaching of the Second Vatican Council."[24] By implication, the law needed reforming because of new experiences. The Committee also emphasized "the oneness of the People of God and universal call to holiness," which demanded that sisters share fully in the mission of the church in the world. While continuing to affirm the value of a life of consecration, the Committee nevertheless underscored that the law should situate religious life within the universal call of all to holiness. They cautioned against any description of religious life that belied its place alongside the People of God. They advanced the proposition that a "variety of patterns of government in religious institutes . . . more adapted to the particular culture and civilization as well as to the spirit of each institute" was essential in revising the code. They noted, too, that the code should recognize "the need for greater flexibility and mobility, for greater openness to the world." And, like true Americans, they cited "the principle of responsible freedom in the decisions of conscience." Applying this to the code, they concluded that "the law regarding religious life must be so formulated as to foster the dignity of each religious . . . and his [sic] growth toward true Christian freedom."

With these and other guidelines for the review of the law, the Committee began with a paragraph by paragraph assessment of the code that involved all the members. They began by identifying canons that ought to be deleted or modified and proposed additions to the law. Then followed three years of detailed study of the existing law. The regions prepared position papers on the major topics covered by the code and proposed alternative canons reflecting their beliefs. At each Assembly the Committee reported to the full membership. Twice the members had the opportunity to review the drafts of sample canons drawn up by Committee members and return their critiques. The final draft (1968) won the endorsement of 95 percent of the members and was published as a copyrighted monograph, *Proposed Norms for Consideration in the Revision of Canon Law* (Washington, D.C.: CMSW, 1968). Mother Omer Downing, SC, then president of the Conference, personally presented the monograph to the cardinal members of the Pontifical Commission for the Revision of the Code. By that gesture she signified how seriously American sisters took the directive that persons should make known to those governing the church their "needs and desires and their opinion on things which concern the good of the Church."[25] The fact that the first project was done without any invitation from church officials did not lessen the women's belief that Vatican authorities would both welcome and incorporate the views of American sisters into the new code.

According to Barbara Thomas, SCN (chair of the Canon Law Committee, 1970–75), *Proposed Norms* became a generally accepted resource at general chapters, and Committee members frequently served as consultants to women's congregations. Like the Sisters' Survey, the work on canon law put sisters in touch with the movements and direction of women's communities in this country.[26]

Just about a decade later, in 1977, the LCWR was asked to prepare a critique of the first draft of the new *Proposed Schema of Canons on Religious Life* (Washington, D.C.: United States Catholic Conference, 1977) prepared by the Pontifical Commission. This time the National Conference of Catholic Bishops (NCCB) initiated the review. The Vatican asked bishops' conferences around the world for their observations on the draft. The American bishops decided to solicit the judgment of the heads of women's communities and include it with NCCB recommendations to the Commission. Although faced with an extremely tight deadline, the Conference's officers and executive director[27] decided to seek full membership participation in the review process. They designed a computerized survey instrument allowing respondents to evaluate every paragraph of the *Schema* in light of ten principles. Five of these were the so-called *principia directiva* (directing principles) adopted by the Pontifical Commission in formulating the draft. The principle of *subsidiarity*, for example (which placed authority for a decision at the lowest level appropriate), was to ensure "flexibility of response to differing church, institutional, social and community needs." An additional five principles reflected values important to American sisters. A *dynamic* canon, for example, "is open to future development and enables an ongoing response to the 'signs of the times.'"[28] The instrument also contained thirteen very focused items to elicit views on such points as whether the proposed law was internally consistent, reflected the theology of Vatican II, and provided for diversity of lifestyles. An open-ended question completed the instrument. Fifty-two percent of the Conference members responded. And two-thirds of these had consulted either the entire governing council or a significant portion of the community. A task force compiled the responses, did a critical analysis of the raw data, and drafted a statement of recommendations to make known to Vatican lawmakers their views on religious life in relation to church law. They wanted to influence the law so that it would be congruent with the experience of American sisters and claim their willing allegiance.

Both these projects forced sisters to evaluate law in reference to the experience they were living. Both drew from the respondents not only the content they desired but the language appropriate to it. The respondents of the sixties consistently sought to validate their recommendations in the light of Vatican II. Having taken seriously the guidelines proposed by the Canon Law Committee, Conference members were compelled, on the one hand, to study the documents of Vatican II and, on the other, to connect the principles found therein with their own experience of religious life. Undoubtedly, this first corporate effort was a catalyst awakening sisters to the discrepancies between the law and their life. It necessarily raised the question of whether religious life is what legal definitions assert it to be or what committed persons live in time and space. It evoked as well a recognition that the law, necessarily universal in its principles, had to provide for national and cultural differences in its application. And *Proposed Norms* showed that even in 1968 American sisters shied away from any final definition of religious life.

By 1977 the women of the LCWR had a much stronger sense of some of the major issues in the ongoing conversation with Vatican officials—sometimes dialogue, sometimes polemic, sometimes battle—regarding the characteristics of the life and identity of sisters. They were also less sanguine about the interest of officialdom in the experience and viewpoints of women and Americans. There was too much evidence of attempts to invalidate the metamorphosis taking place in congregations of sisters in the United States. Between 1967 and 1977 a number of highly conflictive situations developed over questions about the nature of religious life and legitimate expressions of its values. Some were events in the history of the Conference; others occurred outside its bounds but involved it or its leadership. The matter of the IHM sisters of California has already been noted. Inside the Conference there was a sharp disagreement over the bylaws involving the same issues that underlay the Vatican's displeasure with the LCWR and American religious life in general (see Chapter One). Not only some Conference members but church authorities as well believed renewal in this country had run amok. What was emerging was decidedly not religious life. It needed to be stopped.

In this context the critique of 1977, although still animated by the women's hope of shaping the church's law, became something of a last-ditch effort to fend off reactionary efforts to reinstate certain legal provisions that would halt change. Respondents affirmed certain features of the document, the directing principles and the numerous places calling for the individual community to specify its own law regarding a given matter, for example. But they noted that it was not possible to live certain provisions of the law. For instance, "Many congregations cannot be faithful to their charism and mission if they are separated from the world. . . . Rather than separation from the world the canon (93.2) might appropriately insist on living witness to the world." [29] They criticized the document for not reflecting conciliar and later theologies of mission, of church, and of religious life; for requiring hierarchical models of authority; for ignoring legitimate diversities of culture, ideological conviction, and concrete geographical realities (found even within individual communities). Noting that the revised code did not take into account the contemporary experience of the vows, the respondents observed, "The vows are not related to the world and to the conditions of contemporary human existence." [30] Responses also pointed out that the *Schema* was exclusively the work of males and thus failed to reflect the perspectives of women. And, citing the "lived experience" of women religious as a valid criterion for judging the law, the respondents opposed the inconsistency between what the law specified and what women's communities had, over a decade of hard and painful decisions, elaborated in their own community mission statements, structures, and policies. The critical analysis of the *Schema* noted the lack of acceptance by younger members of certain laws, adding that these laws would enjoy a short life expectancy. [31] Significantly, respondents of all ages rejected formulations dealing with the habit, [32] and with amazing unanimity they called for the recognition of women as mature adults. [33]

That a transformation had occurred in beliefs about religious and religious life between the first and second Conference reviews of church law is incontestable. The 1977 critique exposed changes in American religious life within a ten-year period. For example, the women of the sixties were beginning to intuit the apostolic character of religious life; those of the seventies strongly defended it. In 1977 American sisters no longer named themselves "daughters of the Church"; they straightforwardly identified themselves as women in the church. While in the 1960s sisters invoked Vatican Council II to legitimate their viewpoints, in 1977 they relied on the authority of their own experience to ground their critique. They also trusted their American-ness. Values dear to Americans, for example, the right to due process, pluralism, and shared authority, were conspicuous in the critique. As they came of age, American sisters were relocating themselves in the church and simultaneously finding themselves at home in the world, even if at times they publicly criticized it.[34]

As the women changed places, they found a need to justify their altered ways of living and knowing religious life. The two canon law projects provided a framework for the sisters to tackle issues of definition. The starting point for discussion, however, was the law. Received legal norms elucidated by others provided the conceptual construct for the women to explore their own knowledge of religious life. While experience was brought to bear on the knowing process, particularly in the 1977 critique, the framework already in place necessarily set the terms of the exploration. It was two LCWR projects on contemporary religious life that marshaled the common experience of the women and drew from them the language to describe their life and faith. The first of the projects ran from 1976 to 1980; the second, from 1984 to 1987.

The first formal effort to articulate the meaning of an apostolic religious life had occurred in 1971. That year Paul VI wrote *Evangelica Testificatio*, his exhortation to religious communities. Concerned about the use of the statement by some reactionary groups, who interpreted it as a reaffirmation of traditional forms and formulas, the LCWR National Executive Committee decided to sponsor seminars in which sisters could probe the meaning of the statement in the context of their experience of religious life in this country. Several seminar papers were published as *Widening the Dialogue* (Ottawa: Canadian Religious Conference; Washington, D.C.: LCWR, 1974). In the introduction Margaret Brennan, IHM, LCWR president in 1972–73, rejoiced "in the knowledge that women religious were devoting themselves to the ministry of reflection." The book, she said, was meant to serve as a stimulus for further reflection. Indeed, the tenor of the publication was that the papal document should be seen as the first word of a continuing dialogue on what was happening among sisters rather than as a definitive statement settling the questions. In 1973, in her presidential report, Brennan had issued a call for the development of an "integrated apostolic spirituality" that would interrelate ministry, community, and prayer. Conference members themselves, responding to a needs assessment questionnaire during the 1973 Assembly, gave top priority to that call.

In 1976 the membership, acting as the National Assembly, for the first time in its history collectively worked out the organizational goals that should govern the use of Conference energies and resources. Overwhelmingly the Assembly endorsed as a top priority "to set in motion a process to articulate a contemporary theology of religious life consonant with the call to penetrate the world with the gospel message." This goal remains the number one priority of the Conference.

For four years the women assigned to this project, designated the Contemporary Theology Task Force, enlisted a significant segment of sisters in an experiential process of adult learning.[35] Seven questions as devoid as possible of predefined content categories about religious life were formulated by the Task Force to elicit from respondents their perceptions and understandings of the life they were living. Some of these were: "Please spell out one experience you have had which you feel to be a 'religious' experience." "In your experience, what marks you as a religious woman?" "What are the characteristics or qualities of your present experience as a woman religious that you would like to see preserved in the future?"

Appreciating that change continued to occur even as the process evolved, the Task Force believed that change had to be mirrored in the content. When participants objected that the synthesis of responses seemed not to reflect their experience (for example, the concern for social justice was not reflected in the first data), the Task Force introduced additional questions to draw out experience. As specific events, notably the Third Inter-American Conference (1977) and Convergence (1978), the first joint assembly of the CMSM and LCWR[36], introduced new language and theoretical frameworks, the process was expanded to include the new data into the mix. And, even though at various times the Task Force consulted specialists from different disciplines, the data of the project always came from the participants: all LCWR members, a random sample of the general population of sisters, and a random sample of sisters under thirty-five years of age. More than once the analysis of data served as a springboard for structured dialogues in various groups of sisters across the country.

Four publications,[37] each a resource for developing knowledge of apostolic religious life in the United States, came from the project. The last one, *Starting Points: Six Essays Based on the Experience of U.S. Women Religious,* edited by Lora Ann Quiñonez (Washington, D.C.: LCWR, 1980), while pointing out "lines of reflection and guideposts to development," in no way attempted a definitive synthesis of religious life in the United States. In the words of one writer, the essays necessarily have a "tentative ring to them."[38] The data gathered from the women, referring to their own experience and also to shared meanings voiced in collective reflection, reveal that sisters increasingly frame the meaning of their life in terms of the church's evangelizing mission. Clearly evident, too, is their appreciation of a prophetic element in their calling. The sisters strongly espouse an incarnational spirituality, which locates God's action in history.

In the second major project, 1984–87, the Conference resumed its work of articulating the knowledge of religious life as lived by American sisters. Appropriately, the Religious Life Task Force [39] appointed to direct the project strengthened the collaborative features of the earlier undertaking. [40] For American sisters this was a necessary emphasis, valuing as they did the wisdom both discovered and generated through collaborative processes of learning. Relying heavily on collective data, the Task Force carried out a content analysis of significant documents from a random sample of communities (for example, mission statements, administrative reports of leadership groups at the conclusion of their service, and formulas used for taking vows). [41] They analyzed the responses to questions used for the Fifth Inter-American Conference. [42] (One such question read, "From your experience, how have changes in the church and society over the past twenty years influenced apostolic religious life?") They asked all the LCWR regions to reflect on their images of God. Though beginning with personal accounts, these reflections sought to discover whether there was at that time a "communitarian face" of God, so to speak, that sisters shared. [43] In a concluding think tank/writers' seminar, the Task Force brought together several sisters to examine all the data and work it into further questions. The seminar was deliberately structured for intense collaboration (for example, in its modes of interacting and learning and in the style of developing the papers). Prayer and ritual during the seminar were intentionally designed to be experiences of reappropriating collectively the thinking, talking and working that had preceded them. [44] The project's final publication, *Claiming Our Truth: Reflections on Identity by United States Women Religious* edited by Nadine Foley, OP (Washington, D.C.: LCWR, 1988), demonstrates that sisters see themselves as competent to recognize and make public their collective knowledge of religious life.

A number of observations arise from a study of these two projects. In each instance the women were reluctant to suggest that there is but one single valid theology of religious life, much less a definitive one (note the *Starting Points* language above). An image of being on the way, of engaging in a search, stands out in the data. And while the sisters involved in the projects referred to and used theological and institutional tradition, they clearly valued their own experience. For them it was to be trusted as a reliable source of knowledge about what constitutes "religious life" and what identifies women religious. In addition, they saw themselves broadly and deeply in, and identified by, relations with God, the universe, the earth, those among whom they minister, and the human family. Always inclined to look for God in solitude and traditional "spiritual" pursuits, sisters now included "the world," people, the struggle for justice, and the fabric of everyday living among the places where God may be found. The rubric of "consecration" no longer enjoyed the preeminence it once did as the linchpin of identification for both the state of religious life and the women in it. "Consecration" suggested not only a movement away from the stream of history fashioned by human activity but an aloofness and a privileged status many sisters now found distasteful. Too frequently were the concept and worldview on which the term rested used to justify a total immersion in "the things of God" at the expense of "secular" pursuits. Similarly, neither the vows nor the sacraments appeared to have the prominent roles they once played as defining marks of religious life. In fact, the vows were conspicuous by their absence; respondents made few references to them. What was manifestly present especially in the findings of the second project, twenty years after Vatican Council II, were the strivings of American sisters to integrate all dimensions of their life into the church's mission in the world. Involvement in the solution of contemporary problems through institutional and systemic change has become a priority for American sisters. Making their way of life match their professed beliefs is something for which they struggle, particularly in their relation to material goods and worldly advantages. Holiness, now more likely spoken of as "conversion," is increasingly connected with the concrete circumstances of history. For example, the harm caused by prejudice and abuse of power often defines the areas in which American sisters work to be changed in spirit and in fact.[45]

Nadine Foley, OP, in her introduction to *Claiming Our Truth*, capsulizes the reimaging of religious life and of sisters that is occurring in the United States at the end of the twentieth century:

There is an evident convergence around their sense of identity, particularly their claiming themselves as women and their grappling with God images and symbols to fit their emerging self-awareness. These are important developments that fit into a larger context of understanding and of implementing mission and ministry in the contemporary world. (p. 2)

This image challenges the notion that ecclesiastical formulations are the only valid source for information about what constitutes religious life and the identity of women religious. It calls into question a way of knowing religious life which bypasses concrete human experience and its historical grounding.

In 1983 John Paul II directed the American bishops to conduct a study of American religious,[46] particularly the causes of the decline in vocations (that is, numbers of new entrants). Accompanying his letter to the bishops was a document called *Essential Elements*, purporting to be a summary of the "essential elements" of the church's teaching on religious life. Despite some concessions to the evolution of the previous thirty years, its formulations of religious life rested foursquare on "separation from the world."

It was then that the commitment of American sisters to the knowledge they had drawn from the probing of experience was publicly manifested. That year Archbishop John R. Quinn spoke to the LCWR National Assembly, explaining the pope's mandate and his own thoughts about religious life. In response, forty-three members of the Conference spoke to him (and to one another). Sitting on the stage, he heard the women testify to their confidence in the process of renewal that had been underway for twenty years (longer if we accept that the Sister Formation movement of the fifties initiated the search).[47] From microphones scattered throughout the hall, voice after voice placed ministry, the work for justice and peace, and deep involvement in the mission of the church in the world at the core of religious identity. Repudiating the characterization of religious life in *Essential Elements* as alien to the experience of American sisters, they held up the truth of their own experience. Appealing to that truth, collectively shared and reflected upon, the speakers firmly and respectfully declared that change is inseparable from the human condition and therefore inevitably a part of religious life. The air in that hall was electric with energy, pride, and solidarity. The words struck a consistently clear note: for American sisters holiness is undeniably and increasingly connected with the concrete circumstances of history and with their inalienable responsibility to help direct its course. Integrally a part of the church's mission, American sisters will continue to seek their identity and their rightful place in both church and world as participants in that mission (the wellspring of their life). Their words held a consistent message: no one, not even church officials, and nothing, not even ecclesiastical pronouncements, will divert them from that quest. They trust themselves and they trust their journey. Their destination they are willing to discover in the process.

Chapter Three / This Land Is Their Land

AS THE SISTERS WRESTLED with their proper relation to "the world," it was inevitable that other questions would arise. One that surfaced early was the connection of culture and country to religious identity. Sometimes enlivening, often troubling, the issue continues to preoccupy them. Particularly in the past twenty-five years, being American has touched parts of their life once cordoned off as "religious." They have grown to understand that their identity as Americans and their identity as religious are not detachable but interactively related. Indeed, being American—living inside of the conditions that make up the American reality, engaging the events and people that constitute American history, wrestling with the ties between American culture and whatever identity one claims—has been, if not a causal, then certainly a qualifying, factor of the changed identity of sisters as well as the changed dynamic of the life of religious communities. That is, something of the "American character"[1] has entered into the self-understanding of American sisters and into the values and beliefs they own precisely as Roman Catholic religious. And something of the "American character" increasingly recasts their collective relationships with other groups in the church.

Context: The American Quest for Assimilation

Assimilation of and into American culture is not, of course, peculiar to the sisters. It is a major pattern in American history. Wave after wave of immigrants has tackled the challenge of learning the "ways," taking on the attitudes and customs of the country, merging into "we the people."

The Catholics among them labored under a double burden. Ethnic "foreigners" like the others, they were, besides, a religious minority in a nation that, though establishing no religion, had a distinctly Protestant cast. (In the late nineteenth and early twentieth centuries being American was virtually synonymous with being Protestant.) Catholics were thus forced to reconcile allegiance to a church with attachment to their new country. Given the periodic clashes between the tendency of Catholic officials toward moral absolutism and the public's leaning toward moral pluralism (in matters of birth control, for example), the dilemma of the thinking Catholic is never finally resolved. In earlier decades, however, Catholics had to struggle simply to sort out their American identity and to convince others that they could participate fully in the American way of life. To legitimate their religious affiliation they invoked cherished American values like religious liberty and pluralism, the right of free association, fairness, and public dissent. Inevitably they absorbed into their mindset an understanding of government at odds with church polity. A polity in which power resides in the people and is exercised in their name by representative assemblies accountable to the people was (and is) antithetical to Roman Catholic church order. The very principles American Catholics employed to win the acceptance of their fellow citizens aroused the uneasiness of the Vatican. Thus, Catholics walk a thin line between fealty to church and devotion to country.

Although sisters took part in the broader Catholic experience of assimilation, their story has distinctive chapters. In previous decades, once they entered what was known as "the state of religion," the women led an asocial, culturally neutral, existence. Vestiges of European cultures lingered in the lifestyle of communities,[2] and the ecclesiastical culture of Rome also found echoes there. But the ways of religious life were detached from the American experience. The neutral relation to society and culture was a logical consequence of the paradigm that disconnected religious life from the world. It was not so much that sisters positively or openly resisted the culture as that the very structures and rules of their life prevented their coming into contact with it. Ecclesiastical strictures concerning "cloister" and its absolute necessity for an authentic religious life constructed barriers to any enculturation of women religious. Not only were they to be separated from the wider society; their convents were to be "sacred places," off limits to outsiders. Cut off from news about contemporary happenings, forbidden exposure to carriers of popular culture such as radio, popular magazines and fiction, department stores and movie theaters, sisters would not have cited American-ness as a mark of their religious identity. The life of consecration was, after all, above all earthly cultures, its affinities with the reign of God beyond space and time.

Still less would they have appealed to American culture as a source of values relevant to the culture of the community. Distinguishing between members who were "superiors" and their "subjects," drastically curtailing individual choice, subordinating personal aspirations to collective aims (in one community a sister who wrote a book could not use her own name but was obliged to cite the community or a priest as author)—all essential features of religious life—were antithetical to American concepts of equality, freedom, and the right of the governed to a voice. By and large the sisters did not even take part in basic political activities such as casting a ballot. Adding their voices to public discourse would have been unthinkable.

This cultural isolation could not be sustained in contemporary milieux. Some observers of American religious life maintain that had Vatican II not occurred, a transformation would still have taken place in the lifestyles of American sisters.[3] By the mid-fifties the women entering communities were questioning traditional practices. Heads of orders commiserated with one another over the intrusion of the modern spirit into the convent. The new "girls" didn't see why they couldn't continue going to the movies and riding about in cars. They lacked a "supernatural outlook" and seemed more independent than docile. Sisters sent to study on university campuses were listening to the radio and eating in restaurants, activities forbidden back home. Bernard Ransing of the Congregation for Religious told the 1969 National Assembly that the Vatican's document *Renovationis Causam*, on experimentation with formation programs, had been precipitated by many requests for liberalizing rules from heads of orders in view of the change in entrants. While not less generous or more worldly than earlier recruits, he said, they were less mature, less versed in religious culture and church teaching, and accustomed to a high degree of freedom.[4]

Changes in lifestyle were long overdue. By the late forties, the total disjunction between convent life and the wider culture seemed increasingly indefensible. Even Pope Pius XII insisted that sisters update not only their works but their customs in order to be more helpful to modern peoples and that they be educated to a level of competence equal to that of their lay colleagues. His directives called attention to the gap between religious and the very people they intended to serve. The concerted educational movement launched by the Sister Formation Conference precipitated the large-scale movement of sisters out of their circumscribed environments. In substantial numbers they left their cloisters, enrolled in secular universities, mingled with laity of diverse religious persuasions (and none), and tasted American culture through films, travel, and mass communication. Curricula shaped by the SFC introduced them systematically to the social teachings of the church and showed them the linkages among the spiritual, the intellectual, and the professional threads of their lives. Before Vatican II, then, American sisters began to awake to a world larger than their communities, larger even than Roman Catholic turf.[5]

In the sixties the convergence of historical circumstances in the church and in American society accelerated the progress of American sisters toward a sense, not then consciously adverted to, of themselves as Americans and toward the incorporation of certain American values into their form of life. In the first place there was in both arenas a growing realization of cultural diversity and of the influence of culture on the perception and appropriation of experience. In 1961 Cardinal Agostino Casaroli, of the Pontifical Commission for Latin America, put before the heads of American religious communities a challenge and a plea. To save the church of Latin America from the ravages of communism and Protestantism American communities should mission 10 percent of their membership over the next ten years to work in Latin America. Many women's communities promptly initiated or increased the assignment of personnel there. A scant two years later an LCWR survey revealed that, since 1961, 662 United States women religious had been missioned to Latin America. The 55 percent increase was especially remarkable because the increase in the sister population in the same period was only 4 percent. Inevitably, the encounter of sisters with different cultures raised questions not only about methods of work but also about the applicability of certain religious practices. Heads of communities began to hear new messages about the critical need for a degree of cultural relativism in exporting rules and policies. "Each sister . . . must take a basic course in sociology leading to a realization of the *relativity of cultural values* as distinct from absolute moral laws" read a final agreement reached by a meeting of major superiors with personnel in Latin America.[6] The personal visits of community leaders to their Latin American missions gave them firsthand experience of the marked differences in the way people express similar faith convictions.

Vatican Council II expanded that awareness. The very images of the council on television screens gave rise to the inkling that the church, though one, was in fact, not simply in principle, many. As stories of Council debates exposed the diverse, sometimes conflicting, preoccupations of bishops from different regions of the world, understanding dawned that the culture of a people not only determines the forms through which faith is expressed but even conditions the interpretation of beliefs.

In American society similar insights grew. The rising of black Americans to champion their heritage and culture was followed closely by parallel movements among Hispanics and so-called ethnic groups (e.g., Polish-Americans, Italian-Americans). The awakening of Americans to the fact of cultural diversity cast doubt on the long-cherished "melting pot" ideal. Suddenly the cultivation of differences appeared more desirable than their suppression in the pursuit of assimilation. It no longer seemed necessary to renounce one's language of origin, favorite foods, myths, and distinctive celebrations in order to be "American." Thus, "culture" as a category for the analysis of human experience entered the general consciousness of Americans.

In the midst of these events, American sisters were energized and motivated by one Council document in particular. *The Church in the Modern World (Gaudium et Spes)* was to them a clear call for the vigorous engagement of the church with and inside of history. And since they also understood the Council to have placed them squarely within the believing community, whose members all shared the same mission, the sisters felt they could no longer credibly live on the fringes of their times. At the very least they had to know about and try to understand national and international events. Many believed they also had an obligation to enter the contemporary processes of human activity.

The impact of these ideas on American sisters was all the sharper because one of their own was actually at the Council. Mary Luke Tobin, the head of the Sisters of Loretto, was one of a handful of women (the only one from this country) present as auditors in the third and fourth sessions of the Council (1964 and 1965). She was selected because of her very public role as president of the LCWR (1964–67). There is no doubt that the invitation also reflected the importance Vatican officials then placed on the achievements of American sisters. The sisters were proud of her and themselves. They took notice of her experiences. Even before the invitation arrived, however, Tobin—encouraged by other community heads—was on a ship en route to Rome, where she would be readily available just in case the Council members should want to know what American sisters were thinking.[7] On board ship she received word of her selection as an auditor. Besides attending general sessions, she was assigned to the commission in charge of drafting *The Church in the Modern World*. That group was putting together the first contemporary statement by the Catholic church of its commitment to engage in the happenings and questions of the times. Tobin found the energy of the debate exhilarating. It matched the American bent for action. Since the president of the commission, Cardinal John Dearden of Detroit, allowed auditors to speak, she joined fully in the struggle to word this new message. She became steeped in the themes of the document and enthusiastic about its implications for the work of American sisters. On her return from both sessions she became, literally, a roving cheerleader for these themes. She crisscrossed the country tirelessly, bringing the news to sisters in many communities.

One of her strongest messages was that the Council had located the sisters *within* and *among* the People of God (a conciliar image with powerful appeal to Americans). The church now understood that "the joy and hope, the grief and anguish of the men [sic] of our time, especially of those who are poor or afflicted in any way, are the joy and hope, the grief and anguish of the followers of Christ as well." "Christians," said the Council, "cherish a feeling of deep solidarity with the human race and its history."[8] If the whole church was to be both attentive and responsive to world conditions and peoples, even more should the sisters be. For many sisters in the United States the message was a powerful stimulus to and justification for active participation in social processes. The impulse to direct participation came at the very time that the American people were themselves experiencing new public energies. The 1960 election brought in a young president who challenged the people to "Ask not what your country can do for you. Ask rather what you can do for your country." Images of the volunteer in Chile, the activist in Selma, and the idealistic public servant abounded in the media, conveying the power of involvement. Movements of many sorts held up mirrors in which society could take an honest look at itself to correct what was missing in the institutionalization of the American dream. The formation of the Peace Corps, the creation of the Head Start and Model Cities programs, the integration of southern schools and universities, the appearance of the hippy, resistance to the draft, and Martin Luther King's "I Have a Dream" speech introduced Americans to new images of the American spirit and disturbing questions about the American dream. The United States of the sixties was a society questioning long-held assumptions, rewording American values, demanding an effective voice in public policy, protesting war and social injustice, constructing alternatives to poverty, segregation, and war. All those events unsettled, dis-placed if you will, Americans while suggesting other ways of acting out American values. Like the rest of their countrypersons, sisters were being exposed, however unconsciously, to the process of knowing themselves as Americans and testing their biases in relation to American culture.[9]

The Politicizing of Religious Identity

To examine personal and collective images of identity current among American sisters as they enter the last decade of the twentieth century is to mark how American they have become. From acultural conventions of interaction they have moved to patterns and processes expressive of American egalitarianism, openness of purpose, and fascination with the experimental. From a public demeanor that stamped them inaccessible they have moved to behaviors that render them virtually indistinguishable in the public forum. From self-definitions in which consecration for the "strictly spiritual" was the primary category they have turned to self-descriptions in which active presence in social transformation is constitutive of their identity. More significant than the Americanization of overt conduct, however, is the embracing of American culture as one source from which identity arises and by which it is determined. In our view, this facet of Americanization manifests itself most clearly in this reality: American sisters now know themselves, whether individually or collectively, as political. "Political" not merely describes their activities but identifies who they are as religious.

What is it to be "political"? We do not mean being a registered member of the Democratic or Republican party, or even voting in national elections, still less running for public office (though we do not exclude these). To know oneself as "political" is to grasp one's elemental kinship with a "people."[10] It means to discern, however inchoately, that one is *of* the people, which is to say that little in one's life is ever wholly private and that one's most personal spaces have import for the public weal. Beyond knowing oneself in the midst of a people, to be political implies owning responsibility for imagining the common good and for acting to bring it about. And it means understanding one's own people in relation to other peoples, grasping that the welfare of the first is inextricably linked with the welfare of each other people. Thus, the "political" cannot be reduced to very concrete behaviors such as working in a congressional campaign or registering to vote. Rather, to be political is to incorporate into one's self-identification the fact of one's rootedness in a people and to make and act on choices that contribute to the welfare (good journeying) of that people. In this sense, American sisters have become finely political. Whether one concentrates on internal polity or on their engagement in the processes of the larger society, one can observe this change. Today "American sisters" is far more than a geographic tag.[11]

The Americanization of the Conference

The lines of the Americanization process are directly observable in the annals of the LCWR. Like other national conferences, the LCWR was established to provide for the particular needs of religious communities in ways compatible with local conditions. "Our purpose in fostering these organizations on a national or regional basis," wrote Cardinal Valeri, "is precisely to enable those who understand most intimately the particular needs and conditions of their own country or area, to provide for those needs by means best adapted to their situation." And Bernard Ransing, who often interpreted Vatican intentions to the Conference, assured the National Executive Committee that his presence didn't suggest that Rome was "telling you what to do as simply encouraging you to do what you feel is the thing to do for religious life here in America."[12] From its founding the Conference has been unmistakably American (even when its members do not advert to the fact). At times positively viewed, at others considered a mixed blessing, and in more recent years denounced as deviant if not incompatible with the religious aims of the Conference, the American character of the Conference may turn out to be one of its most valuable contributions to the church.

Initially oblivious to linkages between their American-ness and religious life, LCWR members of the last twenty-five years have struggled to come to terms with their American identity. Mirroring parallel developments among sisters in this country, the Americanization of the Conference is, in large measure, the result of its efforts to act in the public forum and to interpret the transformation of religious life in the United States. The imperative to make sense (to themselves as well as others) of what was occurring in women's communities drew forth new ways—essentially political—of interacting and relating to both church and society. In response, members adopted distinctly American strategies—joining in public discourse and dissent, calling for equal access to power, championing the cause of the excluded, and advocating policies to guarantee due process. Thus, in exercising the role, often thrust upon them, of spokespersons for American sisters, Conference members grew to value their social and public responsibilities. They learned how very identified they were with the American dream of an egalitarian society built on respect for the individual, on the right to participate openly in public discourse, on the dispersion of power, and on the necessity of public accountability. Because of their commitment to these values, not only for the United States but for the church and the world, the LCWR is today perceived as an *American* conference, not just a generic church organization of religious leaders.

In its beginnings the LCWR reflected the acultural stance of sisters in general in regard to religious life.[13] The programs of the 1952 and 1961 National Congresses of Religious of the USA, planned by heads of women's communities, took up religious life in the abstract. Topics, for example, of the 1952 First National Congress of Religious of the USA included "Training in the Positive Aspects of the Vows," "Qualifications of Candidates for Foreign Missions," attracting vocations (new members), and maintaining a religious spirit in the midst of "modern convenience and comfort." The themes chosen for programming in the late 1950s were similarly divorced from the American scene.[14] Regional programs of the LCWR in 1958–60 examined "Revitalizing Religious Life," "Holiness in the Apostolate According to the Mind of the Holy See," and "Religious Government." The first of these was broken into subtopics like "Supernatural Foundations of Religious Life," "Recent Directives of the Holy Father to Women Religious," and "Supernatural Obedience and Liberty of Spirit." Except that they were in English, the presentations could have been given in any country. The frameworks within which topics were developed came from general principles of church teaching. Allusions to contemporary culture cited a general culture of modernity rather than the culture peculiar to a local church. And the culture of modernity—judged materialistic, consumerist, and Godless—was viewed as inimical to authentic religious life. Such references to the United States as did appear, for example, in Mother Alcuin McCarthy's report to the General Congress in 1957,[15] were confined to enumerations of the works of American sisters in schools and hospitals.

If the women were unmindful of the American cast of their identity, Roman officials were not. Vatican spokespersons were more apt to allude admiringly to American values and qualities than the Americans themselves, whose earthly city was Rome rather than Washington. Officials of the Congregation for Religious regularly praised American sisters. "The religious men and women in the United States show always and everywhere a strong sense of fidelity, docility, and cooperation with the hierarchy. American religious have an understanding of the . . . perfect way of keeping pace with the times, not by relaxing their rules and living a life of laxity; but by the strengthening of the interior life and by using all the means of apostolate available today in America, the country of opportunities," wrote Archbishop Arcadio Larraona. Elio Gambari, who regularly traveled to the United States to lecture to community heads and formation directors, rarely failed to express his affection for the "dear American sisters," his gratitude for their warmth, and his unwavering confidence in their ability to do anything the church needed. Cardinal

Valeri noted "the special gift for organization which is characteristic of your great country" and the marvels wrought by "close contact and common endeavor," which he considered typically American. Bernard Ransing told the sisters how impressed Rome was by American ingenuity, the openness of American communities to experimentation and change, and the alacrity with which American sisters responded to Roman requests. Even popes praised the Americans. When Angelita Myerscough was introduced to Paul VI at an audience in Rome, he said, "Pius XII once told me that the sisters of the United States are the strength of the Church. And I know it is true." [16]

As the sixties progressed, the LCWR took on the challenges of both Vatican II and the social struggles of the country. Hardly had the Council ended when the Conference tackled with enthusiasm the task of facilitating the renewal of American communities of women. Often without conscious advertence, Conference responses to Vatican II were typically American. The Sisters' Survey and the canon law study were mammoth undertakings requiring organizational know-how and the effective deployment of resources. The Assembly programs of the late sixties combined didactic presentations by innovative thinkers with do-it-yourself presentations of concrete models and practical advice on planning renewal. And explicit references to the American experience cropped up in the reports of these projects.[17] Self-awareness as Americans grew. In 1967 and again in 1968 well-received Assembly speakers urged members to incorporate American experience into their religious identity.[18] "Your special call," said Thomas E. Clarke, SJ, "is to be a channel by which the distinctly American experience of freedom and all that is noble and enduring in it is more fully assimilated into the life of the church all over the world." Indeed, Elise Krantz, SND, complained that whenever a member "tried to get the Conference back on the track" by speaking of the church and of loyalty to its teachings, six or seven other members would rise to the floor to counter: "that isn't important today. We're in America. This is the American church. We're women religious in the United States." [19]

Religious communities had been handed the formidable task of reassessing every area of their lives in light of sound tradition and modern circumstances. Conference leadership, with the concurrence of the members, was determined to provide the information and the exposure to contemporary thought the women needed to marshal community energies for the anticipated change. Although they did not allude to (perhaps did not recognize) the links between their actions and their culture, the process enlisted the very qualities and skills that, a decade earlier, Vatican officialdom had hailed as testimony of the American genius.

Not content to enable change in the individual communities, the Conference, in 1968, undertook a review of its own structures and dynamics. As noted in Chapter One, when the process ended in 1972, the Conference of Major Superiors of Women had become the Leadership Conference of Women Religious. One reason for choosing a new name clearly reflected American political values: "The whole emphasis was to share power and part of the sharing of power was to get rid of the title 'major superiors.' " [20] Internally it had expanded the vehicles for participation of the membership in the election of officers, the choice of goals, and the governance of the organization. It had, in the process, become more egalitarian and democratic, more intent on participating in the time-honored American tradition of social reform. It had recast its mission, situating the development of leadership in its members in the context of the church's mission to the world. It had framed a role for itself in bringing about "constructive social and attitudinal change" (Bylaws, Article II, section 3).

In the late sixties and early seventies the Conference rapidly adopted the practice of taking public positions on and

elaborating strategies to address social problems such as segregation, poverty, migrant farm labor, and amnesty for men
who had evaded the draft during the Vietnam War.[21] Social
justice committees were formed. The National Board sought
NGO (non-governmental organization) status for the Conference with the United Nations as a way of being present to
global concerns. Borrowing Paul VI's words, the 1971 National
Assembly took the theme "The Church Is for the World."
"The Atlanta convention was a stroke of genius," thinks Ann
Virginia Bowling, then a member of the LCWR staff. "The
Atlanta convention seemed to me to be the ideal time to
have settled the problem [of sisters' involvement in social
problems] because once that answer was made, I think the
whole movement towards justice and the whole movement
towards the feminist movement and whatnot . . . you were
free to be able to talk about. But you had to be able to say
the Church is for the world. And I think those who came to
Atlanta still had doubts. I think that convention erased a good
number of doubts in people's minds."[22] From then on, the
annual meetings usually included major presentations and
workshops on the social ills afflicting the country and continually raised questions about the connections between the issues
and religious life (especially ministry). Thus, the Conference
entered American public life, believing, in the words of Mary
Daniel Turner, that "a strong identification with the church is
simultaneously a strong commitment to the transformation of
the world."[23]

Social involvement forged another link between religious
identity and American culture, this one explicit. As LCWR
programs enlarged awareness of abject poverty and its causes,
members focused on the need to do something both to relieve
the misery of the poor and to rectify the structural conditions
that perpetuated suffering. They subjected themselves to un-
comfortable questions about their own complicity in poverty
through the uncritical use of material goods. As the seven-

ties wore on, certain values perceived as integral to American culture were repudiated by sisters as antithetical to their identity and commitment. American culture thus became a foil against which sisters defined themselves.[24] They disavowed the American tendency to define success in terms of material possessions, acquisitiveness, and uncontrolled consumption, which, to many, seemed to generate disregard for the earth, reckless waste of its resources, and competition for wealth at the expense of the poor and weak.

Contact with Latin American peoples in particular and consciousness of the role of American corporations in perpetuating poverty and social marginalization resulted in a growing tendency in the Conference to define religious identity as witness against cultural values and attitudes. In the second half of the seventies terms like "prophetic" and "countercultural" entered the vocabulary used to describe the call of sisters.[25] And some of the qualities linked to religious identity, notably "simplicity of lifestyle" and "solidarity with the poor", derived from a sense that American cultural values were incompatible with the life commitment of sisters. The adversarial posture toward American culture reflected the fact that poverty was the primary lens through which sisters saw (and judged) the culture.

Invaluable sources for studying this posture are LCWR statements to Inter-American Conferences of religious between 1971 and 1985. These occasional gatherings bring together representatives of the Canadian Religious Conference (CRC), the Confederation of Latin American Religious (CLAR), the Conference of Major Superiors of Men of the USA (CMSM), and the LCWR. The first occurred in 1971 when the conferences of bishops and of religious of Latin America convened a group of heads of North American communities. Its purpose was to make the North Americans aware of the problems caused by missionaries from Canada and the United States and to protest the imposition on Latin American situations of practices that they felt reflected North American cultural biases more than religious values. Subsequent Inter-American Conferences were more even-handed. They were jointly planned; their goals and processes addressed shared concerns.

In these forums each conference faced a challenge: to interpret the experience of religious life in its own society and culture and to clarify the effects of a given regional reality on the identity of religious communities. In 1974 the LCWR papers explored the vows in relation to dominant American values. One dealt with religious poverty in the context of a highly critical exposure of American consumerism. The 1977 description of the changing American sisters emphasized how new commitments to structural justice and solidarity with the marginalized stood in judgment of consumerist leanings in sisters' lifestyles. For the Fourth Inter-American Conference, 1980, the conferees undertook to explain the relationship between their respective local churches and the character of religious life. LCWR's paper identified orientations such as pluralism and egalitarianism that had colored Catholicism in the United States and cited issues raised by the connection between faith and culture.

Not only did the Inter-American Conferences serve as a forum for expressing the troubled attitude toward the culture; the meetings fed the attitude. The rhetoric of the Latin American participants frequently voiced the thesis that the economic system of the United States and the trade practices of multi-national corporations were the single most important cause of the mass destitution of their regions. Perhaps more vital, Inter-American Conference schedules always provided for some contact with local peoples and conditions. At the 1974 and 1980 meetings, in Colombia and Chile respectively, that meant walking along slum streets and worshiping with a community of Indians tucked away in a remote planned village. One group talked with poor women who had formed a co-operative to buy staples and who raised small sums selling kitchen towels made of flour sacks. Others listened to the relatives of victims of a government-ordered massacre or shared cake and soft drinks with striking workers and their families. All these contacts set the LCWR delegates face to face with the consequences of uglier facets of American culture. The women felt shaken, guilty.

A powerful boost to the negative correlation between American culture and religious identity (because almost the entire membership shared in the experience) was the 1978 National Assembly, the first joint meeting of the CMSM and the LCWR. Dubbed *Convergence,* the gathering examined the systemic connections between American economic patterns and global poverty. Most of the speakers were from the Third World. Again and again they returned to the oppressive conditions in which the poor live because of corporate and governmental choices made in the United States. Many members characterized this assembly as a "conversion" experience because it brought them to a new understanding of the meaning of social sin, specifically the social sin of their country, and because it forced them to take responsibility for the consequences of American choices. The Assembly adopted a commitment to make decisions in "solidarity with the poor" and raised the now-familiar theme of the level of lifestyle in religious communities.

In two decades the Conference had moved from virtually ignoring culture as a category for the analysis of human experience into participation in American social movements without conscious advertence to culture as relevant to religious identity and then into critical awareness bordering on outright rejection of American culture. In the United States the rise of black and Hispanic cultural pride, and in the church the Vatican Council and growing personal contact with Latin American cultures awakened American sisters to the fact of culture. The affirmation of cultural diversity followed. Later still came the awareness of American culture as a strong determinant of the personal and collective values of sisters and, more central, of their very identity as religious women. By the end of the seventies the dominant stance of the LCWR toward American culture was molded predominantly by the Conference's focus on the world's poor and oppressed peoples. Viewing their homeland from that vantage point, members were at best ambivalent toward, more often harshly critical of, American cultural values. Understandably, a central criterion for judging religious identity had come to be its countercultural bias. If American culture had any role in the identity of sisters at this time, it was as a statement of what they clearly should not be.[26]

All along, however, other currents were present, rarely adverted to and not yet fully usable in the remaking of the American sisters. If they were harsh critics when poverty was the lens through which they looked at culture and society, they celebrated their heritage when the lens became that of power. Ironically the same social involvement that fostered a negative correlation between identity and culture also fed an appreciation of the potential of American political virtues for rectifying social wrongs. When most anchored to its original moorings, American polity assures devices for self-correction. And the women of the Conference invoked these consistently in service of the unincluded—the poor, women, blacks and Hispanics, undocumented aliens, the peoples of El Salvador and South Africa. Assemblies debated and adopted resolutions on farm workers. Members directed the leadership to inform government officials of their concern about Soviet Jews. They demonstrated for peace and against administration policy in Central America. The Conference took advantage of the familiar American do-it-yourself impulse, turning out instructional materials on social analysis, civil disobedience, handling the media in explosive situations, and exploring women's concerns.

Intuitions of American culture as a source of values compatible with the religious identity they were fashioning came through situations in the church. Early in renewal the sisters found themselves in the novel position of being in discord with Roman officials. As the patterns of change became clearer, church officials were alarmed by what they saw as departures from traditional teaching about the nature of religious life and how it should be lived. Even more discomfiting perhaps was the somewhat independent spirit with which American sisters were tackling renewal. In the LCWR the Sisters' Survey and the review of canon law were conceived and implemented without consultation, much less permission, of ecclesiastical authorities. Similarly it was the membership who initiated a rigorous self-study with the aid of management consultants. They made known their needs and their ideas about the services the Conference could provide. On the basis of the Booz, Allen, Hamilton report, they transformed the organization and gave themselves a new name.

By the late sixties the displeasure of Vatican officials at the turn of events among American sisters was making itself felt. Cardinal Antoniutti wrote to American sisters denouncing the changes legislated by the IHM community of Los Angeles. The changes (for example, in dress, in schedules, and in choice of work) by then becoming common in many communities, were completely contrary to religious life, he said. He voiced his anger at the large number of sisters who had written to him protesting the actions of the Congregation for Religious. These sisters were in "serious error."[27]

Antoniutti informed Mother Omer Downing, Conference president, that another Vatican department had scrutinized the 1966 Assembly proceedings and called his attention to "doctrinal inaccuracies" in four of the papers. He noted "tendentious attitudes and a marked superficiality" in the proceedings. The letter closed with an injunction to choose Assembly speakers who were "sound" in their positions and to secure permission before publishing any materials.[28] In 1968 and 1973 letters from the Vatican censured changes in ministry, the absence of superiors in convents, modified clothing, and "purely collegial" forms of government. American sisters were rebuked for failing to seek Roman approval of changes and sternly instructed that the Council's mandate for renewal had not waived the authority of the hierarchy over religious communities. Margaret Brennan, LCWR's president in 1972–73, recounts her efforts to obtain an audience with Pope Paul VI just "to bring greetings to the Holy Father and to bring a blessing back to our Conference." Although the LCWR made the request directly, the Vatican's refusal was conveyed through Cardinal John Krol, then president of the bishops' conference. She pressed him to respond to her questions. "Why did the letter come to him, and why didn't it come to us? And what does it mean [that the meeting] was not advisable?" "He got kind of impatient and he said, 'Well, when you clean up your own house, you might be acceptable to the Holy Father.'" She speaks of all the maneuverings "to bring us in those doors" for meetings with Cardinal Antoniutti." They were just terrible meetings. I think as Americans you always felt somewhat out, like not acceptable because we're Americans. I often felt that."[29]

As the formal association of heads of communities the LCWR found itself playing the go-between. Sometimes the Vatican wanted to use the Conference as a channel to convey Vatican instructions to all communities; sometimes the Conference received official communications on a given subject. Sometimes the Conference was simply the first informed of a Roman move affecting communities. Late one afternoon in 1972, for instance, the general secretary of the NCCB showed up at the LCWR office holding a copy of a letter from the Vatican voicing alarm at the sisters' "abandonment" of the habit. By then the letter was already en route to all the American bishops.[30]

At the conference level, then, the women worked collectively to allay Roman concerns, explain developments in religious life, and try (without evident success) to demonstrate that the changes were not a corruption of religious life. Oddly enough, the women appealed to American political principles—the inviolability of the person, the vindication of rights, due (and fair) process, the public airing of grievances, and the use of dialogue to shape public opinion—when defending to church officials their social involvement and their altered ways of decision-making.

In 1972 the National Board met with Archbishop Augustine Mayer of the Congregation for Religious, who was in the country for the Assembly. The board used the opportunity to explain to Mayer "the unique character of US culture," hoping he would then understand the change in American religious life. They cited the influence of personalism on lifestyle, prayer, government, and ministry; pluralism; and the need for an apostolic spirituality responsive to contemporary needs and the Gospel. They insisted on the importance of distinguishing between secularity (a recognition of and respect for the world and history) and secularism (which connoted a lack of religious faith).[31] Interpreted in a cultural framework, they reasoned, the changes were not deviations from doctrine. They were legitimate variations conditioned—as was true in any country—by the unique experience of a people.

Over the years, as LCWR representatives sought Vatican acceptance of the progress of American religious life, they consistently appealed to culture as a valid source of differentiation in various regions. In the 1980s, as the posture of Roman officialdom toward American sisters became increasingly bitter and punitive,[32] the appeal to culture grew stronger and more explicit. Particularly critical were values such as respect for the dignity of the person, the scrupulous fairness of process required for judging guilt and punishment, the safeguarding of freedom to express opinions, and the distaste for secrecy and covert maneuvering. The cases of Agnes Mansour (whose public service job included administering public funds for abortion) and the twenty-four sisters who signed the 1984 *New York Times* ad on the need for dialogue on abortion taxed the ingenuity of LCWR leadership in rendering accurately and persuasively the influence of cultural values on both the initial incidents and the responses of American sisters to hierarchical retribution. The formal meetings of LCWR representatives with Vatican officials in 1985 and 1986 dwelled extensively on critical facets of American history, culture, and social currents, drawing correlations between these and characteristics of religious life.

The Conference went beyond appealing to American culture in defense of the transformation underway in religious life. At times representatives of LCWR even invoked the same principles in criticizing the polity of the church and the exercise of authority by the hierarchy. Thus, when the Vatican addressed the hierarchy on the subject of the habit, Thomas Aquinas (Elizabeth) Carroll, RSM, then president of the LCWR, protested the lack of prior consultation with those most affected.[33] The Executive Committee would question the Congregation for Religious: "It is not possible, in fact probable, that what in jurisprudence is defined as an experiment is really a necessity of life given cultures and societies?"[34] Repeatedly LCWR representatives asked why no sisters sit on the policy-making body (the plenaria) of the Congregation for Religious. More than once, Conference officers pointed out to the Vatican ambassador in the United States ecclesiastical processes they considered unjust. More than once, they protested the use of secrecy to shield persons who anonymously accused the Conference or individual communities or American theologians or bishops of disloyalty.

A clear demonstration of the growing acknowledgement of the legitimate role of culture in shaping religious identity was the collective speaking to Archbishop John R. Quinn by LCWR women during the 1983 National Assembly. One member after another voiced her dismay at Pope John Paul II's mandate for a review of religious life in the United States. Although the pope's communication to the American bishops in 1983 couched the mandate in language about "rendering pastoral service" to the religious of the country, the behind-the-scenes negotiations preceding the public announcement left no doubt in the minds of Conference leadership that the language of "service" masked the purpose of investigation. Plainly Vatican officials, including those in the Congregation for Religious and the Pope himself, were disturbed by the changes in religious life in the United States and were seriously entertaining the notion of getting American sisters "back in line." They were (some still are) absolutely convinced that the decline in membership could be laid directly at the door of the changes that, in their view, had vitiated religious identity. The women's communities especially outraged them.[35]

When the women flocked to the microphones to address Archbishop Quinn, many of their comments excoriated the *Essential Elements*, the document that the Vatican sent along as a "guide" for the use of the American bishops in examining religious life. Their comments testify to what offends American cultural sensibilities—the voice of the people is conspicuously absent from the document; its approach is ahistorical, nonexperimental; it is an attempt to quell what Rome sees as rebellion; it is an anonymous document, produced in secret; its fuzzy, ambiguous legal force leaves the door wide open for unchecked administrative abuse. A recurrent theme in their remarks was the role of American culture in shaping religious life and the norms governing it.

No one listening to the women could have missed that they unapologetically claimed their identity as Americans and the validity of its impact on their life as religious. "Our American culture is a very alive culture," said one, and "religious life in the United States must be an ongoing living expression of our reality."

Chapter Four / Their Name Is "Woman"

NAMES SIGNIFY. They say something about the thing named. More important, perhaps, they say something about the namer. "The power to name," says C. P. Freund, "is frequently also the power to define. The power to name a group can be the power to position it socially and politically." Noting that a group in search of a new name is often a group in passage, he says of name shifts in the sixties, "Invariably, the rejected name was an assigned one, the substitute a self-definition." "The relationship between power and language," he adds, "is a direct one; whatever the social homilies a society mouths, its language reveals the realities of its power-sharing."[1]

To study the progress of American sisters in the past thirty years is to become aware of the exquisite attention lavished upon naming, more particularly, renaming. As they have repositioned themselves in relation to "the world," they have been trying out varieties of tags to make sense of every kind of experience. New experience has often brought questions about the fit between who they claim to be and what their names are. They have discarded some old names or expanded their meanings; they have made new names.

Not so very long ago bishop and lay Catholic alike spoke affectionately of "the good sisters." With some pride, the women appropriated labels of "children" and "daughters" of the church. Turning adjective into noun, they called themselves "religious." They and others, Catholic and non-Catholic alike, cherished the name "sister" with its connotations of caring and service extended to all in need.

One name rarely used as a marker of identity was "woman." Obviously sisters were females. But that fact had slight consequence in either their own self-perceptions or the notions others entertained about who the sisters were. The classifications used by the church until the mid-sixties to categorize its members bred a certain distance between sisters and other women. Since sisters, particularly in the United States, were by far the largest number of the category "religious" from the late nineteenth century on, the term was virtually an equivalent of "sister."[2] Accurately or not, in pre-Vatican days, "religious" were imaged as a quasi-clerical species, not clergy certainly, but not laity either. Other women were part of "laity" but no one then thought of the sisters as "lay" persons. Hence, there was little basis for the sisters to know themselves as women, still less to identify with other women or their aspirations and struggles.

Furthermore, the spirituality of the century before Vatican II downplayed women and the truths of their experience as irrelevant if not actually detrimental to holiness. Their female bodily features were discounted as immaterial in a celibate life, downright dangerous if not reined in by a vigilant spirit. The internal experience of women—their emotions, imaginings, and thoughts—was suspect. In too many instances sisters assumed these attitudes, which strongly informed their self-perception and behaviors as women. The ideals of spiritual life held up for imitation derived from the experience of holy men and were codified and expounded by male legislators, writers, and spiritual guides. Little in their day-to-day living led them to acknowledge, let alone value, being women as central to their self-identification. Their clothing effectively rendered them neuter in gender. Yards of fabric styled into voluminous habits camouflaged female physical characteristics. Some items (handkerchiefs, undershirts, shoes, watches) were or imitated men's styles. Their hair was hidden, cut very short (in some communities the women were obliged to shave their heads). The expression of emotion was frowned upon, personal relationships curtailed, sexual feelings proscribed. In an interesting parallel to society's almost exclusive focus on the role of mother as the highest expression of "womanly nature," popes and theologians reassured sisters that renunciation of childbearing did not close them off from this exalted function. As "brides of Christ," they took on "spiritual motherhood." The nurturing properties innate to "the gentle sex" could appropriately be cultivated and expressed in ministerial contexts. Perversely, sisters were constantly admonished not to become "attached" to others.

Even a casual observer can see that things have changed. Large numbers of American sisters present themselves as women in appearance. Their dresses look like the dresses of other women; they are as apt to favor yellow as black or navy blue. Cultivating personal bonds is not only permissible but even considered an expression of their vow to be celibate (hence, open and loving to all people). Like other people they enjoy going for a walk or loafing over a hamburger with a friend. Their sexuality as bodied beings early became the topic of workshops and lectures. They are more informed about, more at ease with bodily processes and with their own sexual feelings. Among those whom they trust, they are willing to talk about experiences of closeness with both women and men. To many, caring for the body and looking attractive as women do not seem contrary to a celibate life; rather, being at home with one's body is the mark of a healthy (and holy) person. A bishop chided one sister about her earrings. "Why are you trying to attract men?" he asked. "Bishop," she said, "did it ever occur to you that I enjoy looking good simply for myself?" Like other women they are growing in the capacity to recognize and integrate the experiences of imagination, feeling, and self-awareness. When they draft statements of identity and mission for their community constitutions, they are apt to note that they are "vowed women," "women in mission," "women of the church," "a community of women." Indeed, some church officials who review constitutions complain that the sisters are putting too much emphasis on being women; what should matter, they say, is that they are religious. The community rituals they plan often focus on the faithful women who preceded them—the Sarahs, Ruths, and Mary Magdalens of Scripture, obscure medieval mystics, founding members of the community, the Sojourner Truths and Dorothy Days of American history, their own grandmothers and childhood mentors. Programs for sisters feature women speakers, retreat directors, and consultants. In the public domain American sisters are working alongside others who struggle for equal rights and economic equity for women. They persist in urging civic and church officials to foster responsible, caring dialogue about sexual moral issues and their translation into public policy. They demonstrate outside cathedrals where the ordination of the newest batch of male priests is in progress.

This change represents, in our view, the most critical transformation in the self-identification of American sisters. It merits close scrutiny because it discloses the awakening of sisters to this reality: that the vehicle of their human unfolding is a woman's existence. And this awakening is fraught with layers upon layers of meaning, personal and public. Increasingly attentive to the experience of women as a place where both truth and power abound, sisters have also begun to comprehend that the systems in which they live and work are organized without regard for women and their experience. Of necessity, then, civil and religious structures engender and perpetuate the invisibility and muteness of women.

Without doubt this process, which we call the "feminization" of American sisters, is pluralistic and diffuse. Neither linear nor steady, its course is at times elusive. It is nonetheless real and demonstrable.

What do we mean by "feminization"? In some ways our use of the word appears to validate the "complementarity" school of thought because it implies that there is a body of experience that is, of its nature, "feminine." We do not, however, subscribe to theories of complementarity resting on the premise that there are innate (that is, preordained by nature) gender-specific qualities and roles. Still less do we accept the idea that there is a distinct female "nature." Whether invoked by secular or religious authorities, such notions of complementarity generally function to limit women's choices.[3] That they are sometimes garbed in effusive rhetoric about the "eternal feminine" makes them no less death-dealing.

While rejecting the notion of innate gender-specific predeterminations of human activity (save those based on biological differences), we do recognize that the story of humankind, at least in the Western world, has moved along two separate tracks, each the assigned domain of one of the sexes. Cultural definitions of masculinity and femininity have functioned (and do function) as parameters within which men and women develop identities sanctioned by society. The experiences of women and men thus have tended to be disparate. And differences in experience produce de facto differences in the ways women and men structure reality in their knowing. Consequently, there are traits (gentleness), styles of behavior (dependence, intuitiveness), and roles (helpmate, caretaker) that, while not innate, have been, until now, associated with one gender more than the other. They are, that is, gender-related. While the process of "feminization" we describe rejects the notion that either woman or man is superior to the other, it takes into account that given the course of Western history up to this time, the experiences of women must now be attended to with great care and consciously celebrated as good if equality is to become operative.

American sisters have come to understand that part of their struggle for meaning involves coming to terms with the implications, personal and public, of being women. Far more consciously than in the past they advert to the experience of women. They find truth in that experience and are inclined to take that truth seriously. And they are reaching the conclusion that the best traits and the styles of interaction that women have developed ought to be reflected in social norms, law, public roles, systems, and theories. They should, in short, influence all the policies and structures that human beings create in order to dwell together.

American sisters especially want the structures of the church and of their own communities to incorporate women's knowledge. The experience of women seems worthy of inclusion in official church teaching and theological formulations about religious life as well as the law governing it. The experience of women ought to shape definitions of the status and mission of sisters. The experience of women deserves to figure in norms for judging both theoretical and concrete expressions of religious life. The experience of women is a legitimate source of knowledge about the "givens" of religious life such as ministry, prayer, community, and structures of commitment.

We believe such a process is underway in the United States and that it is a novel circumstance in Catholic history. Only in the past thirty or so years have enough of the necessary conditions converged to enable the recognizing of women's identification and experience. Whether evident to outsiders or not, sisters have been touched by the movements of re-cognition in this country. We do not claim that all or even the majority of American sisters are feminists. Many, in fact, fiercely disavow that name. As much diversity reigns among sisters as among other women in relation to feminist currents. But the majority of communities are feeling the impact of feminism—in styles of worshiping, gathering, ministering, and governing.

LCWR, both as system and as membership body, attests to the reality of the process we call "feminization." In terms of the first, the structures of governance, decision-making, programming, communication, and work manifest characteristics that we tend to identify with women. In terms of the second, the collective body prefers feminized styles of interaction. They vote to maintain the concerns of women as an important piece of the agenda. They identify themselves as women and put energy into knowing their experience as women. They respond to calls to uncover the truth revealed by their experience and to celebrate it. And they persist in trying to translate their new knowledge into public forms, whether civil or church. We believe that one of the critical factors driving the feminization process is that the women, collectively, began to notice the systemic absence and silence of women in ecclesiastical polity, ministry, and cult.

Rescripting the Story: LCWR and Women

Explicit reference to gender-identity in knowing themselves and their organization is relatively recent in LCWR.[4] Certainly self-consciousness as women is not a principal theme of its first two decades. When they insisted on separate conferences for the women and the men, the founding mothers were motivated primarily by a recognition that sisters far outnumbered male religious and that, given the intense concentration of sisters in education, their concerns differed from those of the men (mostly priests). One prescient soul seems to have noticed that the statutes for a joint conference drawn up by the men's committee vested structural power almost exclusively in males. A 1956 draft of the statutes contains a number of marginal comments beside provisions that confer authority to speak for the organization and to direct staff operations on the president of the conference (always to be the head of the men's section). The head of the central office was, likewise, to be a male. Thus, both governance and administration were slated to be under the direction of males. Tiny penciled notes, in what seems to be a woman's hand, exclaim: "even narrower than Canada" (a reference to the Canadian Religious Conference bylaws, which served as the model). Another provision bears the notation: "Only the men's committee?"[5] The inequity did not, however, appear in the public rationales given for separation.[6] The earliest national ventures of the Conference—studies on health care and compensation—focused on problems affecting the sisters in particular, but the reports drew no connections between inadequate pay or health care and gender.

Nor did the sixties bring much change in this area. The energy of that decade welled up from the rapids of change, social and church, that flung the sisters into modernity in just a few years. Out of Vatican II came the promise, greeted with exuberance and resolve, of being actively caught up into the mission of the church in and to the world. To many that promise spelled full inclusion in the church's life, participation with all other believers in the challenge of making the Gospel accessible in contemporary milieux, and hands-on engagement with the significant questions confronting humanity in these times. The women of LCWR poured imagination, resources, and enthusiasm into the task of renewal, anticipating that the sisters of the United States would contribute immeasurably to the life and mission of the church. Hope abounded.

Although the call of Vatican II and the response of the Conference were not framed as issues of women's equality, they nonetheless led to conditions absolutely requisite for the later awakening. In the wake of the Council the women shifted from self-descriptions of "children of the church" and workers carrying out its "apostolate" to new ones of themselves squarely in the midst of the whole People that is the church. To them—as part of the People—Jesus had enjoined the mission to speak a saving word and do a freeing deed on behalf of all creation. That self-image overnight reshaped the sisters' grasp of their place in the church. Among the members of the LCWR, individually and collectively charged with institutional church roles, that self-image elicited both the desire and the expectation to exercise leadership in the broadest arenas of church and world, not just inside their communities. It is clear that they assumed they were now to have a voice in decisions bearing on the common weal of sisters and considerable autonomy to choose community directions. Not only did the premises of the Council lead logically to that expectation. The Pope himself wanted them to be active. Mary Luke Tobin conveyed to them his explicit message:

> It happens sometimes that the horizons of the religious life of women are limited not only in what has to do with . . . this world, but also . . . the life of the church. . . . We wish that the religious woman find today a more direct and fuller participation of [sic] the life of the Church, especially in the liturgy, in social charity, in the modern apostolate, in the service of her brothers [sic].[7]

And, Tobin added, the sisters would be "equal" to the demands of Council and Pope. "Our congregations have pioneered on difficult terrain before; they will not be deterred by the different but not less difficult urgency of this time in the Church."

Moreover, the major projects of the Conference in the second half of that decade—all of them directly precipitated by the Vatican Council—had, it seems valid to say, a strong influence on the members' self-understanding. Participating in the canon law study, the Sisters' Survey, and the reorganization of the Conference gave them, for the first time in the history of religious life, a collective experience of being agents in a field much broader than a single community or diocese. Suddenly they were being forced to figure out what they believed their life to be about and to put those beliefs into words. They shared the experience of marshaling untried abilities. They stood at a rare vantage point. It was almost certainly the first time American sisters articulated common understandings drawn from their learnings.

Reorganization of the Conference in the light of Vatican II set the women collectively to fashioning new structures that institutionalized the values of inclusion, gathering, and self-direction. The search for a new title, which came at the very end, was, in a real sense, almost a byproduct of the intense work crammed into a few years. The change was quite deliberate and in the beginning quite naive. The president voiced her hope that the Conference might adopt a name more suitable to contemporary insights. Several were proposed, one of them chosen. "It was at Atlanta that they changed the name . . . and that was done in seconds," recalls Ann Virginia Bowling. "There was absolutely no debate. Inviolata Gallagher, RSM, proposed changing the name and it went through like that."[8] It was the unexpected objection of the Congregation for Religious to "Leadership Conference of Women Religious" (see Chapter One) that drove the women to tackle issues that groups face when their present name no longer rings true and they are unsure how best to word their identity. When the Congregation withheld approval of the new name for three years,[9] the experience ignited awareness of the relation of identity to power.

From the founding of CMSW to the end of the sixties the women of the Conference were, in a sense, accumulating the experience and the awareness to recognize themselves in later years. A few of the leadership might have linked some of their experiences to the fact of being women, but that was not a generalized comprehension.

The sixties laid down two critical bases for awakening—unfulfilled expectations and collaboration. As the association of officers of women's communities, the Conference poised for full, vigorous participation in the church's life after Vatican II. They expected to have a voice in the church. They expected it because the documents of the Council seemed to promise, even to exact, it. When expectations failed to materialize, they began to grasp that they were invisible in and excluded from the systemic processes of the church. Collaborating in the

Conference further fueled the awakening. The projects they launched to assure high-quality information and thought for the renewal immersed them in the transforming knowledge that comes when the scattered fragments of disparate experience are gathered and its collective meaning recognized. As long as they remained individual heads of individual orders, their experience could only be understood as personal. To comprehend the systemic character of their exclusion required that they come to know one another's experience and recognize the connections. Neither of these movements was framed in terms of gender. Both were necessary for awakening to their identity as women.

The so-called "women's issue" entered the LCWR agenda explicitly when the 1972 Assembly developed the theme *Women in the Church* (selected by the National Board). One of the speakers, Clara Henning, a canon lawyer, galvanized some and shocked many more as she laid out the inequities of church law regarding women. Other speakers urged the women to become attentive to their own gifts as women. The records do not suggest that the papers themselves were memorable or that any one carried special weight in shaping action. But the Assembly put the topic of women and their relation to the church on the shared agenda of the conference. It made the issue public for this particular group of women— giving it legitimacy. That year members adopted a resolution calling for study of the feasibility of LCWR's undertaking full-time research on women. Within two years the Ecclesial Role of Women Committee (EROWC) commenced a short, but indefatigable (and distinguished) life of consciousness-raising, education, and research. Possibly more than any other factor in those years, EROWC kept the "women's issue" prominent. They produced elegant, intellectually stimulating materials that enjoyed wide distribution not only among the members but within their own separate communities. A monograph on the Equal Rights Amendment and on the ordination of women showed women's exclusion to be a question in both church and civil society. A consciousness-raising kit, *Focus on Women*, dispersed far and wide a collection of booklets for group reflections on sex-role stereotyping, symbol and myth as vehicles of sexism, women and God, and the economic status of women. EROWC developed resolutions on women in church ministry and the International Year of Woman and shepherded them to adoption by large Assembly majorities. They saw to it that processes were available for use in regional meetings. Words like "sexism," "the women's issue," and "women's movement" came into the LCWR lexicon. Gradually the members' awareness and knowledge of the women's movements, gender-related issues, and sexism in both church and social settings expanded. And gradually discussions in the Conference began to refer to these realities.

Through much of the succeeding period feminism enjoyed a checkered existence in the LCWR. Without question the Conference leadership played a critical role in sustaining the process. Barring few, officers, board members, executive directors, and staff have persisted in their personal and organizational resolve to wrestle with the tangle of questions posed by contemporary women's movements. And because they had firsthand experience of the power structures of the church, especially at levels transcending a single diocese, they early intuited the linkages between power and gender. Often they have led in identifying and probing related issues. At the same time they have used the vantage of leadership to nurture the possibilities unique to an all-women's organization of discovering and expressing the ways in which women come to know themselves and their world.

It was Margaret Brennan, for example, who challenged members "to understand more responsibly and compassionately the issues that underlie various women's movements and organizations." At a meeting with American bishops, Francis Borgia Rothleubber, OSF, reviewed how the Conference proposed to respond to Pope Paul VI's exhortation on religious life (*Evangelica Testificatio*, 1971). "I was so proud of her," recalls Ann Virginia Bowling. "How could anybody ever not be impressed with this Conference and with Francis Borgia? And when she got finished, Bishop Norman McFarland said, 'I don't understand. How is it possible that women think they could make any response to the Pope?' I got up and left." Theresa Kane, RSM, began with a quiet declaration: "It is fitting that a woman's voice be heard in this place [the National Shrine of the Immaculate Conception in Washington, DC]," and then went on to tell John Paul II "that the church in its struggle to be faithful to its call for reverence and dignity for all persons must respond by providing the possibility of women as persons being included in all ministries of our church." When Francine Zeller, OSF, received a letter from the Congregation for Religious directing LCWR to dissociate itself completely from the First Women's Ordination Conference (1975), she took the matter to the Executive Committee. With their approval and the unanimous support of the Board, she respectfully declined to comply with the directive. Upon the release of the Vatican Declaration on the Ordination of Women, Joan Chittister, OSB, issued a short public statement that the document would not halt discussion on the issue. Then the Board commissioned a special issue of the LCWR *Newsletter* on unclear or contested points. Mary Daniel Turner reproached a committee of American bishops when the first draft of NCCB's response to the Call to Action failed to so much as mention women's status in the church. The bishops' silence on women was especially galling because the proposals about women (from parishes and organizations) outnumbered proposals on any other single topic.[10] Presidents and executive directors year after year held up to Vatican officials the injustice of the church's exclusion of women in worship and governance and defended the propriety of LCWR's concern for women.

Over one and a half decades ago National Boards authorized the first empirical study of women and ministry in the
Catholic church. They directed that LCWR's response to the
NCCB Pro-Life Plan raise the issues of the dilemmas and
needs of women. They formulated guidelines to ensure that
women-related themes were interwoven with the projects on
religious life and social justice. They voted to join the National
Organization for Women boycott of convention sites in states
that had not ratified the Equal Rights Amendment. They
identified the principal themes of LCWR's statement to the
bishop's committee for the pastoral letter on women (1986),
deploring the pervasive influence of patriarchy on religious
thought, symbol, and structure. Four separate LCWR delega-
tions to Inter-American Conferences from 1974 to 1985 introduced the theme of women's experience and of their institutionalized muteness. They doggedly protested instances of
exclusion during the meetings. For example, they objected
to the massive concentration of priests (all men) at the altar,
which left the rest of the conferees (predominantly women)
sitting as virtual spectators. And they voiced their anger when
the sisters were literally evicted from the front row of the
church so the clergy could be seated (the women were assured that they, in turn, were free to bump the layfolk from
their places). And they spoke up when the male presidents
of two of the conferences accepted an invitation to dine with
the Vatican ambassador to Chile and the top official of the
Congregation for Religious, although their female colleagues,
presidents of the other two conferences, were left out.

In the general membership of the LCWR, on the other
hand, a large measure of ambivalence attached to the word
"feminism" and the multifarious realities it conjures up.
Asked to prioritize programs, members tended to give greater
weight to religious life or social justice. Assembly workshops
on those two areas were jammed; those on women under-
subscribed. On evaluation forms of various kinds a number

of voices regularly advised caution in furthering women's themes.[11] Yet, while commitment to name and battle sexism wherever it occurred was far stronger in Conference leadership than in the general membership as a whole during this period, members did support measures (programmatic as well as political) that legitimated the leadership's priority. They passed Assembly resolutions prepared by EROWC. The women they elected to office were persons whose stand on women was public. They took part in consciousness-raising and educational processes. They bought large quantities of the EROWC materials for distribution in their own communities. An overwhelming majority has consistently backed the efforts of the leadership to keep raising issues of justice for women with church authorities. In short, the members not only did not repudiate the leadership's orientation but sustained their mandate to take the women's questions seriously. And they did set about to learn the questions. When it came to support of stands against social inequities among women of color and poor women, their support was unequivocal.

In more recent years feminization has gained momentum in the Conference. Its effects, both hidden and overt, are pervasive. It is reflected in shared language and attentively crafted rituals. It colors the way task groups design learning situations and shapes the women's images of the common weal. It motivates corporate action to bring to many public forums (including the church) values of inclusion, caring, attentiveness to relations, and tenderness for creation. It seeks to collect and make known women's experience and the truths embedded there. It works endlessly to transform attitudes and structures, beginning with the individual communities of sisters.

Now the knowing of selves as women is much more generalized in the LCWR. Collectively the 1984 Assembly voiced a clear call for their own pursuit of a "feminist" spirituality. Grasping that human experience colors our formulations about everything, they seemed to say that the experience of women has a contribution to make to "spirituality"—that is, to notions of the connections between human and divine being and to the search for ultimate meanings.

Indeed all the Assemblies of the 1980s have been notable for their synthesis of women's experience as the *place* where they stand to catch sight of and to interpret life. The Board chose to make the experience of women a focus in the Assemblies of 1983–86. Women as weavers of peace, the journey of American sisters in recent times, women's handling of moral choice, women's experience as a place where the holy can be met—these themes allowed the women to pay attention to their experience and to listen to its meanings. Probing the themes through papers, collective reflection, dialogue, and ritual literally created a school in which the LCWR women could recognize their truth and construct knowledge usable far beyond the borders of women's worlds. The 1986 Assembly was a peak in this movement. The entire program was a process of reflection, conversation, and learning to probe the experience of participants and to look at the glimpses of the holy contained in those stories. There were no keynote speakers or didactic presentations. A team of three women, who occasionally commented on what they were observing and suggested lines of reflection, led the process. Successive steps asked the women to be attentive to the connections among individual stories and to word collective meanings. It also asked the women to allow themselves to articulate those meanings in image and symbol as well as in discursive language.

Increasingly, symbol and myth-making act as major vehicles of meaning during Assemblies. Water jars, strands of yarn, weaving, dance, drama, the blues, the well, wood carvings of the women of Scripture have become as critical as linear discourse in conveying and evoking meaning. The 1981 celebration of LCWR's twenty-fifth anniversary featured an exhibit of work by sister artists and musicians from all over the country. The highlight of the first liturgy was the chanting of the traditional *exultet* (that is, "rejoice") using significant points of the LCWR story as the content of the song. The Gregorian-style chant enumerates the blessings that Jesus's death and resurrection won for humankind. It is used in Catholic services to officially usher in Easter. Using this revered traditional form as the vehicle for a catalogue of special moments in the Conference's story meant the recreation of a powerful religious symbol.

Projects of the 1980s furthered the feminization of the Conference. It undertook an empirical study of Catholic women and ministry and held a special conference to disseminate the findings to persons in key church positions. It set up a joint task force with the National Council of Catholic Women to design materials and a process for reflection on the connections between women and peace. Studies on the current situation of religious life, the exploration of spirituality as women know it, and shared reflections on experiences of God engaged not only task forces but the membership at large. Each of these projects took the experiential knowing of women as the point of departure for reflection and dialogue. Preparation of LCWR's testimony to the bishops' committee for a pastoral document on women and of the material for a discussion of the "promotion of women" with the Congregation for Religious, a day-long board-to-board dialogue with CMSM on the roles of women in the church—these involved the board members, who had ties back to the regions. It was not simply that such activities introduced many members to new content, though that was no mean achievement. They also provided the context for sustained sharing of experience.

Several parallel experiences facilitated the awakening of the women to the linkage between their systemic impotence in the church and their gender. Roughly between 1967 and 1974 a series of events crowded into a brief span shocked the Conference into the realization that, whatever its brave statements, Vatican II had left intact the power system of the church. As individual communities in the United States legislated the changes needed for renewal, it became evident that certain patterns were emerging. They were general trends, cutting across community lines. The Vatican's punitive intervention in the dispute between the Immaculate Heart sisters and the cardinal of Los Angeles, its unilateral decision to launch formal investigations of particular communities (these so-called "apostolic visitations" were usually instigated by the complaints of conservative factions), a rapid series of documents aimed at curtailing more democratic styles of polity, changes in attire, and the autonomy of religious communities in legislating change alarmed Conference members. In written and face-to-face contacts with Vatican representatives the Conference's leadership—and the members in Assembly— expressed strong disagreement with what appeared to them unwarranted intrusions of ecclesiastical power into decisions over which the Council had given the community discretion. They objected further that important pronouncements on religious life continued to issue from the Vatican without prior consultation with the very people most affected. In Assembly after Assembly the members affirmed the same resolution calling for the inclusion of women in church processes and bodies acting on matters that touched their lives. The women were beginning to learn that their expectations of involvement and increased autonomy were not to be fulfilled, but they had not yet made the systemic connections. They believed that if certain key officials were replaced, American communities would find greater acceptance. Most had not yet grasped the link between their institutional invisibility and muteness and their gender.

A few Conference leaders were, however, beginning to make those connections. Margaret Brennan and Thomas Aquinas (Elizabeth) Carroll, for example, became aware, late in the sixties, of the explicit difference in the application of church law regarding cloister to male and female contemplatives. Papal cloister prohibits contemplative women (but not men) from going outside their monasteries. The document *Venite Seorsum* (1969), which purported to address the renewal of contemplative communities, retained "papal cloister" for women's communities. When more progressive American women contemplatives objected to the differential treatment, both Brennan and Carroll pleaded their case with Vatican officials and several American bishops. In a letter to Bishop James Hogan (November 16, 1971) Carroll noted that when the matter of the women contemplatives had been brought up at a recent meeting, both he and Cardinal Carberry took on a harsh tone not evident in regard to any other area. "I feel," she continued, "that in the light of this apparently emotional reaction of men to the problems of the contemplative sisters, it is more than ever essential that women . . . should be involved in the commission on the contemplatives. I feel that there are areas of womanly being and expression that men simply can't understand." [12] And Margaret Brennan and Paul Boyle, CP, noted that in the October, 1972, meeting of the Congregation for Religious with national conferences it was evident that everywhere—not just in the United States—"women want recognition, justice, and equality in the church." [13]

At a 1968 meeting called by three American bishops appointed to study the dispute between the Sisters of the Immaculate Heart of Mary in Los Angeles and Cardinal McIntyre the "upgrading" of the status of women was explicitly linked with the rising tension between the hierarchy and American sisters. One speaker noted that there are segments of both society and the church for whom the "upgrading of women is so threatening that they will fight against the changes being introduced in religious life." Most of the women present were in leadership positions in their communities and in national sisters' organizations. [14]

Whatever the reality about the Conference's relation to feminism, churchmen were convinced that the feminist bug had bitten the women. In terms that anticipate recent fulminations of highly placed ecclesiastics on "radical feminism," Cardinal Antoniutti, then head of the Congregation for Religious, lamented the "erroneous ideas about the promotion of women" of some nuns, which "smothered their natural instinct towards humble and retiring self-giving" (address to superiors general, November 24, 1969). Francis Gokey, SSE, then executive director of the CMSM, wrote about LCWR to the general secretary of the NCCB, Bishop Joseph Bernardin on May 22, 1972. In a "one man to another" tone, he noted that a "limitation" to "prudent action" in LCWR was "a strong thrust for independence which women religious share . . . with all American women today." When the authors interviewed Archbishop Thomas C. Kelly, OP (March 11, 14–15, 1988), they asked him what he believed was the major objection of the Congregation for Religious to LCWR. Without a pause he answered, "Feminism."

Once again, in the first years of the 1980s, the friction between American sisters and church authorities flared up. Individual communities sent their constitutions to the Congregation for Religious for review only to have critical sections (on polity, dress, the institutional control of the community, or forms of work, for example) rejected. The harshness of the sanctions levied against Agnes Mansour, RSM, and the twenty-four sister signatories of the 1984 *New York Times* ad and the absence of due process frightened the nuns (see Chapter Five). A rapid succession of official interventions by the Congregation for Religious into community conflicts (as in the 1960s these interventions often seemed to result from the anonymous complaints of a few) left many with the feeling of being wholly at the mercy of arbitrary power. The very public brushoff of the LCWR members approaching the altar to carry communion vessels back to the worshipers at the

1982 Assembly angered the women and earned them a rebuke from Vatican officials. The 1982 Assembly was a joint gathering of the LCWR (women) and the CMSM (men). During the liturgy on the first day representatives of the Assembly—five women, five men—were asked by the planners to go to the altar at communion time and carry the bread and wine back to the individual tables at which participants were seated. As the people approached the front of the hall, the women were turned away on orders from the Vatican officials who were presiding at the service. Bad as this action was in itself it was more glaring because their male counterparts—peers in position and organizational affiliation—were left as the only ones doing the task. The action occurred in full view of the entire worshiping assembly. No one could fail to make the connection between exclusion and gender. As a matter of fact, many LCWR members, until then sympathetic but not especially devoted to the women's issue, date their awakening to that event. The imposition by John Paul II of a quasi-investigation of American religious (widely interpreted, even by highly placed churchmen, to be aimed primarily at women's communities), the incessant scoldings directed at the LCWR for such transgressions as having non-Catholic speakers, blurring distinctions between sisters and "mere" lay women, using experience as a basis for a theology of religious life, and organizing a procession for peace—all these bombarded the consciousness of the women relentlessly. They were constantly being reminded of their subjection (and expected submission) to institutional officials. And to many it appeared that men religious, especially clergy, were dealt with differently.

Instances of harassment, bullying, and inequality of power are not the only or even necessarily the major experiences that fostered the process of feminization among Conference women. In fact, simply attending to experience, translating it into language in order to share it with other women, and making connections among individual experiences had transforming consequences. Knowing experience as a shared reality became possible as soon as the sisters of the United States undertook to collaborate in areas bearing directly on "religious life" and their identity as sisters as distinct from their role as functionaries in their schools and colleges, hospitals and orphanages. As Chapter One explains, that first collaboration occurred through the Sister Formation Conference. It was the LCWR, however, that brought sisters face to face with religious life as an institution in the church, with generalized concepts of "religious life," with a common awareness of the poor fit between formal church teaching on religious life and the life of flesh-and-blood American sisters. It was the Conference that provided an arena and tools for a collective orientation toward the renewal mandated by Vatican II. It was the Conference that often served as a channel of information and communication about what was taking place in individual communities as they pursued the expectations generated by the Council. It was in the Conference that the heads of communities began to risk voicing to one another their anxieties about Vatican reactions to American developments. It was to the Conference that the women increasingly looked for the education, research, and reflection needed for a new formulation of religious identity. The Conference, in short, was where the women learned to talk to one another. And that talk quite literally gave birth to new women.[15]

It is obvious from the reams of paper expended on publications, reports, memos, *Newsletters*, correspondence, and studies that the women of the LCWR rely heavily on language. Written language is the primary vehicle for communication and education. And information creates a common vocabulary enabling members and their communities to have a shared map of their common country as American sisters. This activity is probably the single most critical factor in the markedly communal quality of American religious life in the past three decades.

Spoken language, talking, is as important. The women of LCWR talk a great deal. National and regional meetings are built around their talking. Talking is the most essential component of board and executive decision-making and of committee and task force work. The annual National Assembly, the one event that brings together an average of 95 percent of the members from around the country, is really an extended conversation. The rounds of eight to ten persons—now virtually *de rigueur* as a seating mode for general sessions—function as primary groups for members. Members want to talk in these groups, complain when there is "not enough time" for sharing. From the groups members rise to speak their word to the entire body in general sessions. Bowling is convinced that the small groups were a kind of training ground where the women found their own voices.

> [There was such value in] having people address questions in small groups, having a voice, those who would never speak to a large group, who never had the courage to. I used to marvel at the increased number each year who had the courage to get up at large group meetings and speak. That growth was really a tremendous growth; not only were you able to speak in small groups but you could address the Assembly of several hundreds.[16]

As Margaret Brennan often says, "The women heard one another into speech."

Talking in LCWR is structured by processes and agendas, by the aims to be accomplished in the group, and by the exigencies of a problem. It happens in response to questions: "Tell about a time when you felt powerless." "What conditions will facilitate this objective?" "What are the themes you want to include in a statement about the Vatican's censure of Charles Curran?" Since 1974 the design of finely tuned processes has been a priority in planning National Assembly programs and National Board meetings. In reality, the processes are varied configurations of talk—reflective conversations with one's own experience and knowledge, verbal interaction in groupings of various sizes, the public dialogue of the full Assembly.

The Secretariat, officers, and board of the LCWR spend inordinate amounts of time planning their conversations with others—with representatives from peer organizations, with church officials, and with publics who must be appealed to. Officers devote hours to the painstaking choice of words to use (or to avoid) in planned meetings with American bishops and Vatican officials. Often the dimly lit basement of the USO—just down the street from St. Peter's Square—became a sort of strategic headquarters for meetings in Rome. There, papers spread all over the orange vinyl furniture, the women would rehearse for hours for an imminent encounter with the Congregation for Religious. They played roles, trying out language. They tagged words that under no circumstances should cross their lips because they evoked such hostility ("team," "empowerment," "dialogue"); others (like "ministry") they would decide to risk, despite reactions, because they thought meanings needed to be expanded. After a meeting with officials they would sit long over plates of spaghetti debriefing, talking yet more, trying to make sense of the experience.

Perhaps, when all is said and done, what feminization has wrought is a fundamental alteration of epistemological frameworks and processes. By grasping the significance of *place* as the vantage point from which one perceives and interprets reality, by grasping the invisible, voiceless *place* assigned to women within social (including religious) systems, by beginning to attend to what they know in the *places* where women live, the sisters have literally come to see different things and see things differently. There is no way women who have awakened can continue to see what they used to see as they used to see it. Many factors may block their ability to change their behavior, especially in relationships. Once awake, however, women inevitably test their voices. And just as inevitably they stumble upon the truth that only new words and new stories will express their new knowing.

Chapter Five / A Rightful Coming of Age

Terms and Themes

AMERICAN SISTERS HAVE COME OF AGE. For more than thirty years now sisters have been at work discovering who they are, what they stand for, with whom they stand, and why. One of their discoveries is that autonomy is not isolation. Quite the contrary. It is to know the self as social, that is, precisely as related. They have come to appreciate that "autonomy-in-relations"[1] exacts choice-making not simply in the privacy of one's heart but in public and social arenas. Gradually, they comprehended that autonomy is fantasy if it does not include being accountable for one's own actions and holding others responsible for theirs.

In our opinion, it is most significantly (though not only) in recasting their relations to the church that sisters learned these truths. Traditionally, sisters received their very self-definition and affirmation from church authorities and prescriptions, sources outside themselves. Coming to grips with their ties to the church as an institution led them, inevitably, to found their identity and, as a consequence, their moral agency on their own inner authority. They learned painfully that they had to separate themselves from their long-cherished father figures, not by severing relations but by establishing in relations the autonomy that rightfully belongs to maturity. Relinquishing accustomed ways of relating to church authority expanded the moral capacities of the sisters, tested their moral confidence, and enlarged the scope of moral claims. Coming of age meant a rightful coming to power.

Maturing in the latter half of the twentieth century, sisters, like others, experienced firsthand that issues are complex, even utterly baffling at times. For Roman Catholics the vision of Vatican II surely ignited this recognition. For the thoughtful of all stripes the social and political climate of the past three decades inflamed it. The moral implications of the Nazi experiment as it related to institutional allegiances, the moral dilemmas posed by the use of the atomic bomb to win a war, the moral crisis occasioned by Watergate, the moral debates (or lack thereof) surrounding abortion, the moral problems posed by contemporary medical experiments, and the ethical issues in corporate take-overs thrust Americans—sisters among them—into uncharted moral territory.

Sisters: Mapping Their Moral Domain[2]

For at least thirty years American sisters have been engaged in moral map-making, creating an ethic and ethos that direct, but neither predetermine nor obscure paths to right action. Like geographic maps, moral maps need on-going review. Traditional modes of discerning good and evil (such as the one that maintains "there is someone who knows the truth and will determine what is good for the community") can and do become inadequate for the task at hand. Norms (like "obedience is simply compliance with the will of legitimate authority") cease to match experience. Once firmly held certitudes (like "adherence to law guarantees righteousness") fail to illuminate new situations. Absolutes become fewer. Whether many or few, however, they require a critical mind and an empathetic heart to render guides for life.

Journeying to a level of moral maturity not typical of them prior to Vatican II, sisters moved to take ownership of their lives and assume responsibility for the common good. Areas of personal choice, in the past viewed as the province of the superior, whose permission had to be sought, shifted virtually overnight to the discretion of the individual. Among these decisions were things great and small—choices about one's life work, dwelling, companions, education, and medical care; choices about bed time, seating order in the dining room, approved television programs, and buying a pair of shoes. Indeed, the classical treatment of the vows of poverty and obedience linked observance to seeking permissions and complying with the directives of those holding some office in community or church. "They shall submit, with pleasure, their thoughts, views, and judgment to the thoughts, views, and judgments of their Superiors," read a typical community Rule. The reason was clear: "It is God Himself [*sic*] whom they obey in submitting to their Superiors." Decisions relating to the common good were the prerogatives of higher authority. The opinion of those affected by the decision was rarely, if ever, sought.

It is inaccurate and unfair to imply that sisters formerly had no moral consciousness and exercised no moral choice. Within the narrowly conceived worldview to which they had been socialized they were unquestionably moral.[3] But, by and large, sisters' choices lay in the domain of the personal. Catholic tradition, after all, has always been heavily infused with injunctions about right and wrong behavior, especially in areas of private morality. The notion of sin—mortal and venial, grave and not so grave—has long played a dominant role in American Catholic teaching and preaching. Every well-instructed Catholic was schooled in determining whether an act was sinful or not, judging the seriousness of the sin, and weighing the degree of freedom present at the time of choice. As noted in Chapter Two, women entering religious communities studied catechisms of the obligations they would incur by taking vows. They were trained in the specific practices that constituted "observance." In addition, sisters were taught that the principles and laws of the church and religious community were fixed. And, sisters were instructed to believe that because directives were mediated by legitimate authority (the unfailing arbiter of God's will) adherence assured moral rectitude. They were socialized to hold a demanding ideal of goodness before themselves at all times. The very labeling of religious life as a "state of perfection" carried strong overtones of perpetual vigilance over the rightness and wrongness of choices.

The scope of moral choice extended to interpersonal and professional matters also. Sisters made judgments about their relations to community members, superiors, students, and patients. Sisters in administrative positions—principals, college presidents, hospital executives, and superiors at various levels—had to make judgments about matters beyond the purely personal. Observers have noted that it was in ministry settings, actually, that sisters had the opportunity to exert the autonomy of adults, in contrast to the dependence and docility expected in the convent. Instances abound. The administrator of the large teaching hospital not only ran the institution effectively but dealt with her peers in the field and with civic officials. The college president oversaw governance, finances, and curricula. The scholarly anthropologist conducted field research with grant funding. The high school drama coach staged the annual musical to which an entire town flocked. All these women then returned to the convent, where they had to ask permission to stay up past 9 P.M. and where their lives were governed by the regulations of canon law and community custom.

As Chapter Two indicates, the contrast made perfect sense in the context of the traditional concept of religious identity that distinguished between "religious" life and "apostolic" life and between primary and secondary or essential and accidental elements of the religious state. In such a framework, the work sisters did was an adjunct to religious life, important, but peripheral. The difference between the autonomy and creativity legitimate at work and the dependence and passivity sanctioned within the convent did not strike anybody, especially sisters, as incongruous. Seldom did the question find its way into theoretical discussions about religious life.

Morality had an institutional face as well. For example, the interaction between a religious community and the institutional authority of the church was characterized by the same dependence, reliance on permission, and compliance with externally defined norms. Canon law, hierarchical decree, and the word of an authority constituted the normative framework for making judgments. A legal prescription or the directive of a church authority, simply by its existence, exerted a claim on the community's conscience. There was only one permissible response: compliance. If the community leadership believed that a given prescription was inapplicable in a particular situation, they requested an exemption (for example, for the community to expend a large sum on a new hospital wing). The norm itself, however, was not disputed. And if, after all attempts, the exemption was refused, then conforming was automatic.

Standing up to an individual authority was not unknown in earlier history. One group of sisters abandoned their brand new headquarters on the day of its dedication rather than accept the restrictions the local bishop wanted to impose on their ministry. And several community annals contain accounts of a sharp-tongued mother superior who flatly refused to bow to a bishop's orders. But such disputes were rarely on the level of norm or teaching. By and large, the sisters, collectively, received the dictates of church authorities on doctrine, moral code, and discipline as formulations of "the truth" binding their conscience and choices. It would not have occurred to them that definitions of the "nature" of religious life, regulations governing individual behavior, the conduct of community affairs, were suitable matters for disagreement, much less for noncompliance. Not likely to think of the church in terms of institutional power, systemic relations, jurisdiction, and rights, they were even less likely to image their relation with the church in those terms. The sources of legitimate norms against which to make decisions tended to be outside themselves—God's law expressed in the Ten Commandments (as interpreted by ecclesiastical authority), church teaching, canon law, the directives of the Pope and the Congregation for Religious, and the orders of the local bishop. All these came from the church; other sources (scholarly findings, for example) bore little relevance to morality.

Vatican II, in particular, turned upside down this narrowly circumscribed and precisely defined moral worldview. Challenged to look at both the church and their calling from an entirely new vantage point—the mission of the church in the world—sisters had to alter radically their ways of seeing, judging, acting, and relating. They had to expand the domain of their moral responsibilities. Though personal goodness was indispensable for moral integrity, sisters were sensing that it was simply inadequate for the renewal of religious life mandated by Vatican II. The complex sets of interaction of persons among peers and with others produce a corporate personality having its own moral character. The interaction of relations, especially systemic ones, generates an ethos enhancing or bankrupting the moral life of the community. As a consequence, sisters were beginning to comprehend that moral agency requires something more than a privatized code of ethics. Shifting from the individualized understanding and practice of morality that had traditionally governed their lives and work, sisters moved to create a social, public ethic. They gradually situated themselves within the human community in its various configurations—their country, women, the poor, and the people of the church.

Repositioning themselves in relation to the world had no little impact on their ties with the church. The security they had known as moral minors, dependent on others for their moral choices and actions—and for approval—did not serve them well in new experiences. Norms had to be drastically reshaped. No longer could prescriptions founded in narrowly determined premises about "authentic religious life" evoke their allegiance. No longer could they settle for laws in whose making they played no part. No longer did it seem credible that decisions of authority, simply because they were decisions of an authority, should have a claim on their conscience. Rather, from their newly situated place in the world as well as from their newly found freedom in their own communities,[4] sisters came to believe they had something to say in the formulation of church teaching. Consistently they now seek a hearing in the forums of ecclesiastical power, wanting their perspectives weighed seriously in episcopal decisions. They question a great deal. A few even refuse to comply with legislation or directives they perceive to be misguided or downright mistaken, such as the prohibition against political involvement by sisters. They believe that the primary responsibility for determining the mission and direction of a community belongs to the community. They assert that they have a rightful role in making church law on religious life, and that, as a matter of fact, not every area of their lives should be regulated. The work of communities on their constitutions and their endless struggles with Roman authorities to have the constitutions recognized testify to these convictions.

This change is apparent in LCWR. As a corporate moral person in its own right, the LCWR perennially engages with other corporate agents that, though external to and separate from the Conference, wield valid claims on it. Especially salient is the fact that the members of the Conference hold positions systemically defined and regulated by the Roman Catholic church. Although officially excluded from the polity of the church, the leaders of women's communities are linked by law to the hierarchical authority system. By virtue of position and roles, the formal leadership of women's communities routinely have firsthand contact with the men in positions and roles of authority. They are, thus, placed in situations where they can more easily awaken to the systemic structuring of relations in the church, in particular its power relations. And the women of LCWR attend carefully to the ethical significance of actions. The stories they share among themselves are apt to be stories of moral striving.

LCWR: Mapping Its Moral Domain

When we use terms like "moral agency," "maturity," and "moral choice," we do not claim that these are the women's words. As we examined the data yielded by written record and oral story, however, we were struck by the resonances between the women's experience and the copious accounts—popular and scholarly—of adult moral development, in short, of "growing up." Further analysis convinced us that, whatever the language of the sisters, our observations are grounded in their experience.

In our judgment, it is the cumulative effect of the diverse forces at work within and outside the Conference rather than single incidents that have matured the Conference. Surely the moral integrity of the founding women, the creative spirit of the refounding members, the quality of the elected leaders, and the stamina and vision of the membership as well as the competency of the national secretariat over the years have all played a part in the coming of age of the Conference. The projects undertaken, the programs sponsored, the research carried out, the interactions with other groups and organizations, and the change and conflict that sometimes accompanied and followed upon these activities were not indifferent factors in the Conference's learning the many lessons related to growing up. Each in its own way contributed to moral maturation. And, while we certainly recognize that some forces and factors played a more dominant role than others (for example, rewriting the statutes, taking public positions in political matters, and constructing corporate theological reflection on religious life), we believe there is a fundamental connection among these various realities. We think every chapter of this book discloses the multiple influences at play in the moral growth of the LCWR.

Since its inception, the women of the Conference have invested energy and resources in formulating the identity and mission of the Conference and their own identity and mission as church leaders. The recurrent scrutiny of statutes, bylaws, and resolutions is evidence of this. Each of these tasks has involved examining their relation to the myriad situations making claims on them. The deliberate and regular identification and evaluation of Conference goals and priorities testify to the weight they give to this responsibility. In clarifying identity and mission, they have realigned themselves, and thus the Conference, in relation to those on whom they previously depended, especially those in positions of authority in the church. For example, responses to Vatican directives concerning the habit make it clear that the major superiors did not acquiesce simply because authorities pronounced something good and necessary. Letters of Thomas Aquinas (Elizabeth) Carroll, RSM, and many others reveal an unflinching posture in the face of the treatment accorded the Immaculate Heart of Mary sisters in California by churchmen. Action on behalf of cloistered sisters also made apparent that when directives from Rome are viewed as unjust, the Conference (in most instances, the leaders of the Conference but supported by the members) was not silent.

Their automatic acceptance of received norms has shifted. On the one hand, they are more apt to scrutinize the pronouncements of authority and to accept or reject them on the basis of their credibility and persuasiveness. Their response to the 1983 *Essential Elements* amply demonstrates this fact.[5] On the other, they are far more creative and active in constructing norms for judging situations and options for response to those situations.[6] In other words, they take on themselves— as a facet of moral agency—the responsibility to share in the framing of the norms to which they give allegiance. Such publications as "Board of Reconciliation and Procedures for Due Process in the Religious Community of Women" (Washington, D.C.: LCWR, 1972) and "The Religious Significance and Canonical Dimensions of Issues of Separation" (Washington, D.C.: LCWR, 1974)[7] as well as a manual for social analysis are examples of Conference efforts to enable members to devise processes and norms for making sensitive moral decisions.

While taking seriously the tradition of the church and the body of its teaching, they have enlarged the sources they take into account in determining a course of action. For example, they accept cues from the unincluded voices whose experience usually does not figure prominently in the formulation of moral teaching. One striking instance is the document *Choose Life* (Vivien Jennings et al. [Washington, D.C.: LCWR, 1977]). Its introduction reads: "The National Assembly in 1972 adopted a resolution to encourage our sisters 'to become better informed on matters militating against the growth, development, and preservation of life.'" The 1973 Assembly adopted a similar but stronger resolution. It stated that the Conference is "to commit itself to the development of a deeper and more honest understanding of the right to life issue in its broadest implications as it affects all oppressed persons." The authors of *Choose Life* further amplify its purpose:

> We see as our purpose in this paper to raise consciousness of women religious around the pro-life issue; to offer pastoral and educational implications of that issue in the context of related quality-of-life-questions; and to support future agendas by which religious communities, institutions, and church leadership can respond more effectively when the problems in this issue are met not at a level of theory but in the lives of persons who are in pain. (p. 3)

Needless to say, this position was not well received by the National Conference of Catholic Bishops. It and LCWR were, in fact, publicly attacked.

In summary, the membership evidences a markedly evolved consciousness of the moral dimensions of human experience and of their capacity for forming moral judgments. They more readily appropriate the power ethical decisions and behavior require. They act, assuming their role as adult moral agents in both church and world. And, as owning their American-ness made them aware of the political dimensions of their commitment, and assimilating their gender identity enabled them to take hold of their womanhood, maturing in moral agency sensitized them to the "sociality," the rightful "autonomy-in-relations," that moral maturity exacts. As a result, they consider themselves full members of the church with the right and the obligation to take part in shaping its identity, framing its legislation, and deciding actions in view of its mission.

Each facet of this corporate moral agency deserves elaboration in its own right. The task is too large for one chapter, however. Because the approval of church authorities, indispensable for the Conference as an official church organization, plays a key role in the coming of age of the Conference, we single it out for examination.

The loss of approval is a terribly disturbing possibility to many in the Conference. In our interviews with Conference leaders they all spoke of the fear they felt in dealing with Vatican officials. They dreaded, as it were, the impending extinction of the Conference for failing, in the minds of officials at the Congregation, to meet its obligations as a "church" organization. It is as an official organization that the Conference not only experiences the benefits of its public status, but also feels the use of raw power, tastes its own powerlessness, and encounters ecclesiastical interference. In redefining the mission of the Conference, in deciding its relations, and in giving account of its activities, the members of the Conference, particularly its leaders, come face to face with the fact that the Conference lacks any real legal standing to determine—even in mutuality with church authorities—the identity, purpose, and relations of the Conference. It appears that the very institutionalizing of their role as major superiors under the auspices of the church leaves the Conference without any recourse when relations are not just or fitting.

Collectively, the members of the Conference have had to deal explicitly with this reality. Gradually comprehending the consequences of their nonstatus in the polity of the church, they wrestle with their unwitting complicity in this situation. Too long willing to be treated as minors, "children" and "daughters" of the church, the leaders of women's communities have been repositioning themselves in relation to those on whom they had grown dependent (and who like them that way). As happens in other groups that seek their legitimate autonomy, the recognition of their unwholesome dependence stirred the moral energies and imagination of the leaders of women's communities. And while certainly not the only factor in the Conference's becoming a powerful corporate body, the recognition of their indentured state undeniably had the effect of mobilizing, at first with some reluctance, the moral agency and corporate power of the Conference.

Language about the leaders as moral agents is not like the terms "American" and "women" of the previous chapters, terms the Conference invoked consistently over a decade or longer. The theme of American-ness, implicit from the beginning, surfaced overtly in the early seventies; the theme of women entered the official vocabulary of the Conference at about the same time. References to moral reasoning and decision-making, subjects of attention in their own right, are more recent additions to the collective vocabulary of the LCWR. Actually, an objective framed by the National Board in 1984 called for programs to develop the competence of Conference members and their communities to make moral judgments. The objective reads, "To raise consciousness among the membership about the need for formation of conscience; increase our understanding of what moral choices are." Arising in a long-range planning process, this objective reflects the Board's awareness that in both society and church moral questions were increasing in complexity. Solutions were fraught with ambiguity, their repercussions far from clear. Increasingly, it seemed, decisions carried with them, among other things, the threat of right-wing pressure and Vatican sanctions. The formal training sisters had received in the past often proved inadequate to the tasks of responsible choice now proliferating in hospitals and social agencies, city councils and political campaigns, community assemblies, the LCWR and international forums. The Catholic church itself, at every level, was the scene of debate about personal and corporate options whose rightness or wrongness was far from evident. That direct allusion to moral reasoning and moral choice entered the collective language of the Conference later does not mean, however, that the experience it points to is just now appearing.

By the late 1960s Vatican officials were beginning to sound a theme that would be fully articulated only in the 1980s, the issue of "competence." As a legal term in the juridical system of the Catholic church, "competence" refers to the legitimate scope of action of an ecclesiastical entity, organization, or group. What is legitimate is determined by its "proper nature." The nature of such bodies is, of course, defined by legislation of the church, even though the rhetoric of Vatican officials usually leaves the impression that the "proper nature" of such groups—for instance, religious communities or national conferences—is an act of God and exists in its own right. (Were that the case, a legal formula would not be a human construct but simply a rendering of what already is.) One thing is certain: an entity itself may not, on its own authority, change its nature. That is solely the prerogative of church officials. The issue of "competence," therefore, has presented no small challenge as the Conference, over the years, assumed more and more responsibility for its own identity and legitimate autonomy, eschewing the notion of a fixed nature for a living organization.

Frequently, Vatican officials assert that the LCWR takes on agendas that are, baldly put, none of its business. They do not, that is, fall within the class of activities in keeping with its identity as a conference of heads of communities. Matters pertaining to "religious life" (for example, the vows or prayer) are within their province, but not secular issues (like racism) or those bearing on the teaching authority of the church. The LCWR's persistent opposition to United States policy in Central America, its pursuit of social and economic justice for women, its carrying out of a public procession for peace (Pentecost Sunday, 1982), and its efforts in the Mansour case to convey to church authorities the harmful impact of their procedures are examples of activities considered illegitimate. (Agnes Mansour, a Sister of Mercy, was forced to choose between her membership in the community and her work, approved by the authorities in her community, because the Michigan department she was to head distributed funds for abortion. She chose her work.) Consistently, the Vatican reprimands LCWR representatives for its "disloyalty to the magisterium." In taking public actions and making decisions at variance with ecclesiastical positions, the Conference incurs the wrath of Roman officials. For example, LCWR contributed fifty dollars to the 1975 Women's Ordination Conference and adopted a resolution supporting Charles Curran, an American theologian censured by the Vatican.[8] At times reprimands are accompanied by thinly veiled insinuations that the Vatican just might strip the Conference of its official approbation. In violating its "nature" defined by law and interpreted by the "Holy See," the Conference does not deserve its official status.

The consistent response of LCWR representatives to the

accusations and reprimands has been to explain and explain and explain why the contested activities are in keeping with the nature of the Conference and the nature of religious life—why, in fact, they are demanded by moral obligations. Explanations appeal to pastoral needs (in Guatemala, for example), church documents (such as *Evangelii Nuntiandi*), the distinction between interpretation and observable fact, the role of culture in perceptions and value judgments, and, above all, the Gospel. The Conference has been unflagging (and not only when under attack) in its efforts to interpret American sisters and religious life. It seizes almost every opportunity to present the thinking of the leadership of women's communities on the call of apostolic sisters, the nature of religious life, and the identity of the Conference as an ecclesiastically recognized organization. From the early seventies to this day, the Conference has reported on varied aspects of religious life in this country, for instance, the role of sisters in political ministry, new forms of polity in religious communities, the use of new ways of missioning sisters, developments in formation programs, and the process of approving constitutions. An unintended effect of the ceaseless attempts to explain, clarify, and vindicate the activities of American sisters and of the Conference to church officials, here and abroad, has been the strengthening of the moral capacity of Conference women.

Ironically, it was the church, especially the Vatican, that actually handed the leaders of women's communities a critical vehicle for becoming morally aware and pro-active. The association of communities and sustained intercommunity contact and discussion were necessary prerequisites for sisters to experience a generalized perception of religious life in this country (as distinct from knowledge of their own individual communities). That is, the personal experience of the individual had to be seen as part of a social, systemic reality. The founding of the Conference offered a context for shared analysis and reflection on matters new to the leaders of communities of sisters, namely, religious communities and American sisters considered collectively. It provided an organized forum for knowing corporate identity, sisterly solidarity, and collective decision-making. Intercommunity association also heightened the likelihood of corporate action, and, thus, the eventual discovery of corporate power. Especially in American culture, when people work together in a sustained relationship, they gravitate toward wanting to act on problematic situations or for desired change. This was especially true when, in the very early years of the Conference's life, Vatican II charged religious communities to update, leaving nothing unexamined in their lives. Roman officials urged the Conference to take an active role in this endeavor, while respecting the autonomy of each community. Probably without either the sisters' or the church officials' realizing it, the Vatican advocated the very conditions needed for the exercise of corporate power, that is, melding the autonomous and relational dimensions of maturing moral agents.

Coming together as a national conference was thus indispensable for the moral growth of these women. From its founding, members were brought face to face with issues of ownership. In designing the statutes, as has been noted earlier, they took full control. They considered and acted on questions concerning the common good—for example, giving priority, at least initially, to regional rather than national needs. They determined organizational policies, among them the dispersion of power within the Conference and the form of their relation to other organizations. From 1962 on, they worked at institutionalizing contacts with church authorities in the United States and the Vatican, seeking to prevent ruptures and to safeguard communion. They focused on efforts to establish structural relations with the National Conference of Catholic Bishops, annual visits to Rome to confer with Vatican officials, and measures for reconciliation with the Consortium Perfectae Caritatis.[9] Work on committees and task forces provided members experiences in acting jointly, discovering their likenesses and differences, struggling to deal with them, sorting out what was conducive to the common good, and presenting to church authorities their informed judgment on a given issue. For example, the Conference projects pertaining to canon law and to the theology of religious life represent deliberate efforts to take charge of constructing new knowledge about religious life and its meaning while not screening out differences. Through the work on church law members collaborated in trying to institutionalize their views of religious life without making absolute any one view. Through the contemporary theology projects the women attempted even more. Assuming the initiative in articulating new theories of religious life gathered through corporate reflection on experience, they were in effect putting the emphasis on empowering themselves, individually and collectively. To secure official approval of their views was not their primary object. Comprehending their own diverse views was.

The pursuit of collective ends thus gave Conference members a sense of corporate power. In the late sixties, as Chapter One outlines, the Conference took a fresh look at itself as an organization. Believing themselves responsible for framing and acting on the mission of the church in the world, the leaders of sisters' communities were convinced that the Conference had to be assertive. It must invest itself in fashioning a church faithful to Gospel values, responsive to the concrete historical reality, and capable of offering alternatives to unjust systems and practices. "Participation in the transformation of the world" [10] became, as it were, a consuming passion of leaders of American communities. Establishing a Peace and Justice Office and securing non-governmental status at the United Nations in the early seventies are indices of the Conference's new orientation toward the use of corporate power and moral agency.

At approximately the same time that the Conference was

involving itself in secular affairs, the nuns at large were defining themselves as politically responsible. Of necessity, then, they thought of themselves as having institutional power in American society. And use it they did. The American scene gave them ample opportunity to immerse themselves in movements to achieve clearly defined aims—end the Vietnam war, secure amnesty for conscientious objectors, wipe out segregation, guarantee civil rights for minorities, vanquish poverty, place certain people in office, and keep others out. Participating in these movements, sisters tasted their power and figured out how to use and share it. They were learning how to develop strategies to ensure certain outcomes for the common weal.

Their activism in public affairs caused no little ferment in women's congregations. They evoked grave concern on the part of church officials as well. And officials translated this concern into efforts to stem sisters' increasing involvement in the secular sphere, more accurately, to control, even stop, their acting "in the world." The rubric of "consecration" served as grounds to declare certain ventures out of bounds. Sisters, and certainly the leaders of women's communities, belonged in the convent (as other women belonged at home). Thus, the experience of sisters in church affairs was the exact opposite of their free participation in civil arenas with its accompanying exercise of moral agency and collective power. As a result, community heads, individually and collectively, came into open conflict with church authorities. They learned how differently Rome viewed sisters' newly found sense of the church's mission as it relates to them. They saw how differently church officials judged what were for American sisters values of the Gospel, not simply political or cultural practices. Enlarged participation in civil spheres, the exercise of power to secure one's purposes, the right of self-determination, and the worth of each individual's contribution were finding their way into the ethos of religious communities. The same experiences were becoming more and more a part of the moral fabric of the Conference as well.[11] The opposition of Vatican and American authorities to these developments hastened the awakening of the women leaders to the fact of their institutional exclusion from and their impotence in the polity of the church. In time, the intransigence of the church as a system became an undeniable catalyst for the Conference to lay claim to its moral authority and offset ecclesiastical measures to domesticate its spirit and public activities.

That 90 percent of American communities of sisters are associated in and through the LCWR guarantees that questions concerning the relation of women's communities to the church are probed collectively. Especially during the seventies and the eighties the members grappled with the fact that church officials did indeed want to circumscribe if not rescind the autonomy sisters thought they had been granted by *Perfectae Caritatis* and *Ecclesiae Sanctae*. Forced to confront the extent to which their power and its use depended on the sufferance of church officials, the membership dealt with the question of whether, in fact, they had any real institutional power in the church or, for that matter, even in the affairs of their own communities. In particular, Rome's response to the constitutions of many communities conveyed a disregard for the corporate authority a community believed itself to possess. Especially under fire was community legislation on participative government and the responsibility of sisters to share in decisions affecting their lives. Repeatedly, the leaders of American communities experienced that in actuality they had no legal recourse when they judged their rights to be abridged by church officials. To be without legal power or to have its limits determined without any say on their part, or, worse still, to have no redress in real or perceived injustice wounds the moral sensibilities of sisters. Comprehending the injustice of their situation, they have gradually exercised their moral agency. Every chapter in this book contains examples.

No one event, no chronological series of events, no one person, nor many persons taken collectively account fully for this steady movement in the Conference. But in the 1980s, as the posture of Roman officialdom toward American sisters became increasingly hostile, the maturing of the Conference became more public, more explicit. Particularly critical to the moral passage through which they were moving were certain values, such as respect for the dignity of the person, the scrupulous fairness of processes for judging guilt and punishment, the protection of freedom to express opinions, and the distaste for secrecy and covert maneuvering.

The 1984 Assembly illustrates well the corporate coming of age of the Conference. During that meeting the membership assumed "competence" in an area traditionally reserved to church authority. Several months earlier the National Board had discussed at length the increasing incidence of Vatican intervention in and censure of American communities of sisters. The Board reached the conclusion that the entire Conference membership needed to reflect on the experience and its meaning. At the Assembly the president, Catherine Pinkerton, CSJ, laid out, in a measured but forthright presentation, the pattern of Vatican action. She spoke of some of the cultural and ideological differences that seemed to account for continuing official suspicion of American sisters. Two members shared publicly the stories of their interaction with Vatican officials. The two, a Franciscan and a Benedictine, had been asked to tell their stories. They described the situations and reflected on such questions as: "How did you experience the event?" "What facilitated or handicapped your handling of it?" "What would have been helpful to you in this situation?" "What issues do you think need to be probed?" As the women spoke, audible gasps greeted some details. Even members who were generally loathe to criticize church officials were aghast and communicated their reactions to the president in person, in their comments at the floor mikes, or on their evaluation forms. The full Assembly then discussed and voted on two resolutions asserting the legitimacy of Conference assistance to communities in conflict with church officials and authorizing the leadership to establish resource panels to help members in such situations. The two resolutions passed by lopsided majorities of 463–3 and 462–4.

The members directed the Board to act accordingly when the need arose. Their action was an acknowledgment that the lack of structures for due process in the church did not dispense the Conference from finding ways to compensate for this deprivation. And even though such actions have no legal stature, they would be a sign of the moral commitment of the members to one another. Sisters must stand together when truth or justice appear to be at risk, not in opposition to church authorities but in solidarity with one another. Asserting simply that it is right to create support for those deprived of a fair hearing for perceived or real injustices, they promised companionship knowing that their solidarity would be misunderstood, even condemned, in some circles.

Major issues of the maturation of American sisters as moral agents are concretely expressed and synthesized in the case of the twenty-four sisters who signed the 1984 *New York Times* statement on abortion. The situation heavily colored the 1985 National Assembly. LCWR members entering the Assembly hall beheld a huge black-and-white drawing at the front of the room. On it were the figures of three women, water jars on their heads, striding toward the three-dimensional model of a well on the stage. One could be excused for imagining that they were moving toward the other women, the sisters filling the hall. *Women at the Well* was the program title, women as moral decision-makers, the theme. Two major papers, "The Moral Decision-Maker: From Good Sisters to Prophetic Women," presented by Anne E. Patrick, SNJM, and "From Moral Insight to Moral Choice: Discernment and Decision-making in the Christian Community," presented by

Margaret Farley, RSM, provided the conceptual frame for the women's work.[12] For four days they literally put themselves through Moral Reasoning 101. Asked to bring to awareness their own beliefs about moral agency and choice and to evaluate them after each theoretical presentation, they spoke their thoughts to one another, puzzled over differing convictions, and participated in workshops on contemporary situations demanding complex moral analysis. The exercises were not purely academic. The women had to tackle some immediate real-life questions related to the involvement of the LCWR in the aftermath of the *New York Times* ad.

During the United States presidential campaign of 1984 several American Catholic bishops, including a couple of well-placed cardinals, used their ecclesiastical office to castigate the Democratic vice-presidential candidate, Geraldine Ferraro, for her stand on choice relative to abortion. Many Catholics were outraged. They perceived the action as a blatant intrusion by the hierarchy into the election process. The bishops' attacks on Ferraro had the practical effect of publicly aligning them with the Republican candidates, creating the impression that no good Catholic could in conscience vote for the Democratic ticket. The total exclusion of other issues, such as poverty, civil rights, and nuclear proliferation, as criteria for assessing candidates and parties caused indignation among these Catholics.[13] In an attempt to restore the balance, close to one hundred Catholics signed a statement published in the *New York Times* as a paid ad. The ad noted that recent statements of American bishops left the impression that there is only one "legitimate" church position on abortion. It stated that, in reality, a pluralism of positions on abortion exists in the Catholic church. It called for dialogue on the issues embedded in the abortion dilemma. The use of the term "legitimate" evoked the wrath of church authorities. Its un-nuanced use was certainly one factor but not, surely, the only one that contributed to the bishops' opposition to the ad. Among the signatories were twenty-four sisters.

Early in December, 1984, the heads of their communities, all members of the LCWR, received letters from the head of the Congregation for Religious instructing each to secure "a retraction" from the signer in question. Should the person refuse to recant, the community head was immediately to initiate procedures to expel her from the community. Several recipients of the letter contacted the LCWR National Secretariat at once, asking for help in convening as a group as soon as possible. Once the Conference officers had authorized that assistance, those who had initiated the request contacted their colleagues from other communities with signers, inviting them to a meeting. Before the end of January, 1985, three meetings had taken place.

These first meetings—held within a four to five week period—enabled the participants to exchange information and examine the issues. Together they developed a shared perspective on the legal questions, identified options, and evaluated them in order to make their individual decision with as much clarity and responsibility as possible. The exchanges also allowed the women to express their thoughts and feelings, and to be mutually supportive. At times they talked about the collective experience of the group. As the situation evolved, they became more critical of their own decisions, especially when these seemed to exacerbate tensions. For example, a joint agreement about limiting information to the press earned them the reproof of sisters who would have preferred a sharper public confrontation with church officials.

It was always clear at the meetings that each woman retained full autonomy in relation to the signing members, to the individual community, and to church authorities. It was also clear that no one could make binding commitments on behalf of the governing council of her community. No one specific procedure was ever adopted, or even proposed, for resolving the cases. At the same time the women kept sight of the interconnectedness of American communities of sisters. A strong awareness that the decisions of individuals had widespread implications persisted throughout the process. The group continued to work together until the middle of 1986.

From the beginning, the president, vice-president, past president, and executive director of the Conference were included in all the meetings.[14] When the group selected a steering committee from among themselves to coordinate communication and future meetings, they deliberately included the LCWR president, Margaret Cafferty, PBVM, for her analytical skills and objectivity. During the meetings the LCWR representatives were often resources on the workings of institutional church structures and the styles of particular officials. As a quasi clearinghouse the Secretariat was in touch with the reactions of the press, colleagues in other denominations, the concerns of the LCWR membership at large, and peers in other Catholic national organizations. The staff could thus offer insights on the general ramifications of issues or strategies.

More than once, the officers laid the situation out to the entire National Board, who gave time and thought to the matter from one perspective: its potentially harmful impact on sisters and religious life in the United States. While the Conference had no official role in the individual cases, it did have a legitimate interest in the common welfare of women's communities. The ad and the measures taken by the Vatican raised critical issues affecting all communities. Although these issues had been addressed at one time or another in the life of the Conference, they were now more precisely formulated. They included, for example, the collision of local and Roman cultures, the linkage between the choices of individual members and the collective accountability of the community to society and the church, the structural relations between community authority and hierarchical authority, the clash between ecclesiastical preference for secrecy and the very American penchant for public disclosure as a means of keeping parties honest and protecting individuals against abusive institutional power.

The arena of institutional church authority exacted several roles from Conference leadership. Within days of the first phone calls from community heads the officers and the executive director met with the Vatican ambassador in the United States. The women wanted Vatican officials to understand that their action was alarming large numbers of American sisters. It heightened their disaffection from the institutional use of authority in the church. Further, it was important that officials understand that an unsatisfactory resolution of the conflict held the potential for polarizing the sisters, triggering a rise in exits from communities, and discouraging new entrances. Perhaps most critical of all, the women underscored that key elements of the processes employed by church officials in this case were abhorrent to Americans—the presumption of guilt without an opportunity for self-defense, the preemptive determination of sanctions to be inflicted, and the bypassing of the individual sister and the legitimate community authority. These struck Americans as unjust. In addition, the law of the church seemed to lack safeguards for individual and community rights as well as avenues for redressing abuses, perceived or real.

If Conference spokespersons broached these issues with the Vatican ambassador, Archbishop Pio Laghi, they struggled mightily to communicate them to the head and staff of the Congregation of Religious at formal meetings in 1985 and 1986. With these officials they explicitly put forward the thesis that personal and collective moral choices are made within the context of particular cultures and social traditions, not simply in relation to abstract sets of laws and norms. Understanding and judging such choices must take into account cultural values and symbols. Dissent, for example, is not, in American culture, the heinous offense that church officials judge it to be. Repeatedly the LCWR officers advanced their belief that a culture and its symbol systems play more than a casual role in shaping the conscience of a community. The Gospel requires as much—a human, incarnational ethos directing the moral agency of a people.

The 1985 Assembly not only provided a forum for the LCWR members to hear an account of the Conference's association with the fallout from the ad, but offered a situation in which the members had to confront a problem involving them. One of the main speakers, Margaret Farley, RSM, had signed the *New York Times* statement. Her standing in the eyes of the Vatican remained unresolved at the time of the Assembly. The Conference officers had been pressured for months by both NCCB and Vatican officials to withdraw their invitation to her to speak. With the concurrence of the full Executive Committee and the support of the National Board, the officers refused to do so. They believed that repudiating Farley would be unjust. She had been through no due process; her guilt had not been established. To levy sanctions against her would simply be wrong. For a public body like the LCWR to cancel the invitation would injure her good name, to which she had a right. Archbishops John R. Quinn and Pio Laghi then rescinded their acceptance of invitations to celebrate the liturgy and to speak at the Assembly. To be present, they felt, would discredit them in the eyes of Vatican authority, damaging their efforts to cultivate among Vatican officials a more positive image of American sisters.[15]

Having laid out these matters to the National Assembly, the officers solicited membership questions and reactions. Members were asked to participate in extended role playing, each person in a work group putting on the behavior and wrestling with the attitudes of a party affected by the *Times* ad. Members found themselves trying to think and speak like a local bishop, a signer, a feminist, an anti-abortion activist, a journalist, and a community leader. The exercise concluded with small group debriefings and an at-large Assembly discussion. Members had to put into language their internal experience of putting on a stranger's mind and formulate moral questions the situation raised. They formally registered their opinion on the decision not to rescind Farley's invitation. Overwhelmingly members supported the officers' decision. Those who disagreed or had reservations were almost exclusively preoccupied with the implications of disobeying or displeasing the hierarchy. Some felt that refusal to comply with the directives of church authority is simply and of itself wrong. Others struggled over whether noncompliance could be reconciled with a commitment to unity and peace. Some shrank from the thought of inflicting personal hurt on Laghi and Quinn, especially the latter, who was trying hard to forestall any harmful outcome of the study of American religious then underway at the initiative of the Pope. The participants collectively experienced that in complex moral situations no alternative guarantees a happy ending. The situation brought stark opportunities for taking responsibility for one's action and its consequences.[16]

If the *New York Times* ad with its attendant circumstances and consequences taxed the moral ingenuity of all involved, it also tested the moral confidence of sisters in church officials and polity. It most certainly made clear that American sisters decide their own interpretation of which matters are appropriately within their competence. It laid bare the norms operative among them in making moral judgments. It revealed that self and autonomy, relatedness and norms, concrete situations and principles of church teaching, all carry weight in moral choice.

Thus, the *New York Times* debacle suggests that community leaders found in this experience an appreciation of the complexity and the ambiguity of moral choice. They had to accept that it is not possible for even the most conscientious of moral agents to know 100 percent innocence. Some signers, for example, perceived themselves to be excluded from the deliberations of their leaders; some felt that the leadership had been co-opted by the institution; some protested the absence of the press at the meeting; others judged that the Conference was speaking for them rather than with them. Efforts to clarify these perceptions were usually unsuccessful.[17] The women learned that figuring out how to put all the factors at work in corporate moral agency into some kind of honest interplay does not guarantee blamelessness. Avoiding all mistakes in judgment is rarely achievable in such a situation. Certainly there are constants in the moral juggling act—like trying to take multiple viewpoints seriously; granting each viewpoint its due as a chip of the truth; communicating that rejection of a viewpoint is not meant to injure the dignity of its holder; safeguarding the rights of all parties; achieving, wherever possible, consensus; preferring public, open discourse rather than secrecy; and taking care to prevent ruptures. But the configuration of constants has to be created anew for each and every decision. It has to be judged on the merits of its unique fit to each and every issue under consideration. Even with such care the rightness of any decision and its positive effects for others is not assured.

This story illuminates the critical facets of moral agency for an individual and an organization. It discloses the corporate moral growth taking place in the Conference. Obviously, it dramatizes some of the more serious moral dilemmas of the 1980s. But most significantly, we believe, it uncovers the moral terrain—the complex social, ecclesial, and political issues—that needs moral mapping as sisters journey into the twenty-first century. Exposing the magnitude of the moral tasks ahead, the *New York Times* ad and its unforeseen consequences also suggest that still further journeying awaits the sisters in this country—especially as publicly recognized church women.

Chapter Six / Not Without Struggle

AT THE LAST DECADE of the twentieth century, communities of American sisters differ strikingly from themselves at mid-century, when change was just beginning to stir. Then their ranks were increasing, climbing steadily[1] to over 180,000 by 1966. Today, in the early 1990s, they number about 128,000. Then a reassuring proportion of the members were younger women. Today only 1 percent of the sisters are under thirty. Then they were concentrated in an impressive array of institutions—colleges, hospitals, parochial and private schools, orphanages, homes for the elderly, and clinics in foreign missions. Today they are dispersed in a variety of ministerial settings, far more ad hoc and transient.[2] Then the members of a community wore distinctive uniform attire, marched to the same clockbeat in patterns recurring daily, monthly, and yearly. A common set of required prayers, practices, and rituals governed religious discipline. Observance of rules and customs, of schedules, of superiors' injunctions and church discipline was the external sign of a "good religious." Today the women exhibit diverse dress and dwelling. The spiritualities and theologies and styles of worship they pursue are legion; they expend time and energy in tailoring forms of prayer to situations and participants. Then very clear lines of command rested on premises about hierarchy, the mediation of God's will through authority, and personal autonomy as inimical to holiness. Today ideals of participation, equality of access to power, and the inalienable responsibility of each person for self and common good drive communities to continue remaking their structures.

As we've noted earlier, the highest authority of the church, an ecumenical council, mandated systematic adaptation and renewal in religious communities. Within ten months of the Council's ending, a second instruction spelled out criteria for the task and a deadline for communities to get started. "In each [community]," it stated, "in order to put renewal and adaptation into effect, a special general chapter is to be summoned within two or, at most, three years."[3] Vatican directives used the words "experiment" and "experimentation" to describe the search for new ways. To American sisters those were dynamite words. They implied a trial and error approach. They suggested discovery of the truth through experience rather than application of universals already defined. In fact, in a society like the United States, "experiment" inevitably exploded into a way of thinking about religious life that departed radically from earlier paradigms. And—for the sisters of that period a truly critical factor—it seemed to come with the blessing, even the command, of church authority.

With alacrity sisters set themselves to the task of reimagining apostolic religious life and of learning whatever was needed to acquit themselves well. One has to have lived in American women's communities during and just after Vatican II to know the energy and ferment, the exhilaration, and the sense of fresh possibilities that saturated the air. In the church many events promised the kind of change that would completely reinspirit belief and behavior. And there is no question but that the social tenor of the times in the United States accelerated the momentum of change in religious communities. The sisters were not only surrounded by events that were turning the country inside out; many were actors in these events. Significant, too, was the rapid founding of new national associations at the grassroots level by sisters between 1968 and 1973. The National Assembly of Women Religious linked religious identity and social activism. The Sisters NET-WORK registered as a lobby to bring to bear the church's social teachings on Congress. The National Black Sisters Conference and Las Hermanas focused on racial and ethnic issues within religious communities. In the experience of organizing, sisters discovered and invented new ways of doing old things (advocating grape and lettuce boycotts, for example) and new things that needed doing (like influencing the investment policies of banks). In the experience, as Chapter Two makes clear, they constructed new religious meanings.

Particular changes were not the only subjects of debate. Eventually, necessarily, change became an issue in its own right. Church authority said that change must be restricted to "accidental" and "secondary" elements of religious life. Under no circumstances were communities to tamper with the "essential" and "primary" elements. It was inevitable that both sisters and hierarchy would eventually have to tackle issues of the nature and species of change, whether a change left intact the "essence" of religious life, and even whether the historical character of human existence did not call into question the very notion of "essential" (therefore permanent) forms. This discussion has not ended.

A central point of the argument is the *kind* of change that has occurred. Some see the changes that have taken place as a radical perversion of the nature of religious life and the result as a mutant. Others maintain that the changes are simply a natural outcome of reclaiming the vision of community founders; they challenge the adequacy of categories used to analyze the nature of the change. Still others insist the changes are merely modifications enabling sisters to respond to the contemporary world precisely in fidelity to both the Gospel and the rich variety of founding inspirations. Without the changes, they say, religious life would depart from its true nature.

We characterize the changing of American sisters as a transformation of religious life, a veritable redefining of its properties and a reidentifying of the women who live it. We believe the transformation, still in progress, is altering not only experience but epistemology—worldview, concepts and categories, language, ways of knowing, and meanings. For many communities the transformation has also been a revitalization. These communities have managed to rediscover and relanguage their myths, capturing something of the original spirit that energized founding members. A number of communities, for example, have mounted major research into primary sources about their earliest days. They have invested prodigious ingenuity in connecting community myth with the contemporary environment, and community tradition with the questions that engage humanity now. One group of communities has banded together to reinterpret the meaning of "Providence" in relation to current global issues such as ecology. The altered consciousness of many communities has led them to reclaim founding women once tacitly consigned to obscurity because they stood up to bishops. Their sense of incorporation in the mission and the believing community of the church (as distinct from its polity) is strong. Individual members are marked by a far more conscious sense of identity than was possible fifty years ago. And they are working hard for a shared identity whose vigor does not depend on the distortion or the destruction of personal or corporate integrity.

In examining critical facets of the reidentification of sisters, each of the preceding four chapters introduced the theme of conflict. And, indeed, conflict has played a major role in the change. That should have been expected, though it was not. Change of such magnitude, accomplished at such a fast pace, is fraught with conflict. A movement of such drastic proportions rearranges not only concrete experience but the internal frameworks and processes through which experience is internalized and interpreted. It literally bombards people's sense of themselves and of their life's meaning with issues of critical import. It dislodges them from the places, carefully fashioned and tended, from which they have been accustomed to relate to themselves and the being that surrounds them.

Although the movement of change began to take shape well before Vatican II, conflict became a major dynamic after the Council. Both consequence and catalyst in the movement, conflict played the role of partner in a dialogue, a dialectic with change.

Handed their orders to change (and to move expeditiously enough to be able to revise their constitutions by the end of ten to twelve years), many American communities lost no time in getting started. As we noted in Chapter Two, they took quite literally the dicta of *Ecclesiae Sanctae*. They were struck by several charges in particular. Communities themselves had been given "the main responsibility for renewal and adaptation" and told to leave no facet of their lives unexamined. General chapters were to bear the lion's share of directing the renewal process, and the whole community must be consulted in preparation for the first special chapters.

Preparatory discussions, hearings, and studies to identify the areas in which the community needed change were, in most communities, the first opportunities in memory for the sisters to interact as peers in weighty corporate matters. And the special chapters were, possibly, the first truly representative bodies in the modern history of women's communities. That is, they probably had more truly grassroots people than ever before. Gone was the covert pressure of former times to select delegates from among local superiors. Agendas reflected the concerns of the members at large as distinct from previous agendas composed of issues the top leadership identified as needing attention. Chapter delegates often consulted the membership at large through forums and open discussions while the special chapter was in session. And that membership kept a watchful eye on chapter deliberations.

Thus the renewal chapters were historically the first opportunities for the membership of a community to discuss important matters openly and the first opportunities for them to disagree (and to realize that they disagreed) on fairly substantive issues, including religious beliefs. Because of the intense energy surrounding the special chapters (and one or two subsequent chapters) the stakes were perceived in terms of "all or nothing." In that context conflict was particularly sharp, readily generating bad feelings. Sisters were then neophytes in handling overt conflict, reaching consensus, and distinguishing idea from proponent. They sometimes fought "to the death." And perhaps there was something of death in the air—the death, on the one hand, of a way of life that to many represented not only security and certitude but also conviction and, on the other hand, the death of passionately embraced hopes if change were to fail.

Conflict took on a life of its own as a force directing the course of renewal. The expression of divergent, sometimes mutually exclusive, positions (on political involvement, for example) forced proponents to greater clarity of articulation and to a determined search for facts and principles to substantiate their position. The more persons and groups invested in pursuing a line of discourse, the greater the investment of their selves in that line. Such discussions were not purely academic but usually a prelude to decisions about concrete actions— for example, making living arrangements, using personal discretion in spending money, and decision-making. Decisions were often freighted with consequences, such as whether or not a community would continue its schools. In such contexts, "winning" was all. Inevitably, then, positions often hardened quickly, lines were drawn too early, and closure sought prematurely. If this situation was serious within individual communities, it was doubly so when the divergence was between the Conference or a community and the hierarchical authority of the church. In such cases, the nuns feared the changes they so passionately wanted were in mortal danger, and the large-scale renewal they imagined would be aborted. In the earliest years of renewal, conflict was colored by a kind of panic, some seeing all that they cherished and had given their lives for disintegrating rapidly and others seeing all their dreams of newness facing extinction before they could even be born.

Conflict, in turn, generated further change. Conflict drove proponents of differing viewpoints to scrutinize their values, their beliefs. To strengthen the acceptability of their thinking to others, they invoked shared foundational beliefs. They refined strategies to ensure that the policies they favored would pass. Inevitably, their adherence to certain positions intensified. Doing all that work and probing underlying beliefs confirmed them in certain orientations. When conflict rose from disapproval of choices individual members were making, about housing, dress, ministries, and leisure activities, it often strengthened the resolve of both the disapproving and the disapproved to persist in their ways. The confirmation of people and groups in their own viewpoints and choices solidified their pursuit of change.

As ecclesiastical authorities began to censure the direction change was taking, conflict among the sisters took on an institutional, even a theological, dimension. That is, for those who equated "the church" with institutional authority, positions were not simply matters of opinion among peers. Positions were not matters of opinion at all. Their validity did not rest on the persuasiveness of rationales. Rather, the matter had already been settled in advance because the voice of authority decreed which was the correct choice. For some that translated into which choice was God's will. But this approach gradually carried less and less weight among members who had accepted Vatican II formulations about collegiality and subsidiarity, the participation of the faithful, and the equality of all believers. To the extent that these women also owned their moral responsibility as adults, their freedom of conscience, and their identity as women, they could not acquiesce solely because authority said so. They were obliged to subject directives to their own moral reasoning.

When, besides, their positions and choices were assailed as "disloyal" and "disobedient" to the church, "contrary to its teaching on religious life" and, worst of all, contrary to the will of God, the women felt their very integrity impugned. They had, therefore, to strive harder still to demonstrate that their values not only were compatible with Catholic religious tradition but restored that tradition to its primitive spirit. They appealed to the Scriptures and to reams of church documents to authenticate their stances. They were thus grounding themselves in the most serious framework of meaning they could have invoked. Furthermore, the flat-footed techniques (like pounding on tables and making sarcastic remarks about the appearance of a nun in ordinary dress) used by certain Vatican and American bishops to express their disapproval and rein in the sisters were distasteful to many as Americans and as women. Episcopal behavior and language that were perceived as just plain churlish and arbitrary helped to undermine the very positions advanced by officials of the church.

Through the LCWR experience we can get a close-up view of the change-conflict dynamic of the past three decades. It is important to underscore once again that the Conference is not a religious community. The women belonging to it do not come from a single historical tradition. They have not entered into a permanent commitment to the LCWR's mission and values. And, obviously, the Conference does not encompass every aspect of a member's life. Topics that might appropriately make their way onto agendas of community chapters, like ministry goals, housing policies, or guidelines for dress, are not suitable topics for Conference action. The Conference was and is, however, an actor in crystallizing and clarifying trends in American religious life. It has played a major role in organizing the sisters' experience of religious life and the way they think about it and in attempting to interpret this to the hierarchy of the church. Its members, particularly its officers and governing board, have been active players in the movement of change and its attendant conflicts.

In the Conference the change mandated by Vatican II took off quickly and purposefully with the Sisters' Survey, intended to facilitate the planning of change by providing solid empirical data about the population asked to do the changing.[4] The findings of the Survey were presented and discussed at the LCWR Assemblies in 1967 and 1968. Concurrently, the Canon Law Study was launching the leaders of communities into their first venture in scrutinizing church law and framing criteria for its revision. Conflict did not lag far behind. Some of the members regarded the survey instrument as subversive, giving harmful ideas to the sisters at large and causing them to doubt traditional positions. In addition, Marie Augusta Neal's use of the terms "pre-Vatican" and "post-Vatican" to categorize the orientation of respondents toward change offended several members.[5] Questioned about her choice of language, Neal explained that the prefixes "pre" and "post" were meant simply to convey chronological facts.[6] Items labeled "pre-Vatican" came from documents written prior to the Council; the others from documents written during or after the Council.[7] That is not how they were interpreted. To many members, the terms implied a judgment; more conservative members felt cast in an unfavorable light. One member contacted Neal immediately and threatened to discredit the Survey unless at least four theologians stipulated by the member corroborated the validity of the differentiation. Neal secured the required number. Three concurred with the classification of items, the fourth referred the question to a colleague, who also concurred.[8]

The Canon Law Study, too, gave rise to conflict. In 1967 (the year of the first reports on the Sisters' Survey) regional subcommittees assigned to research specific areas of the law reported to the National Assembly. They relayed the main points of the position papers written to support their recommendations to the Canon Law Committee. The two California subcommittees revealed that "an honest difference of opinion" existed between them on formation (socialization of new members) and profession (taking vows). In dispute was how much latitude individual communities should have to determine their own policies and programs. The northern subcommittee felt that it was the Vatican's prerogative to retain primary control and that canon law ought to spell out requirements in detail. The southern group found that position untenable because it effectively elevated the code of law into a fixed "prototype." That position, they thought, presumed the code was the sole correct formulation and any departure was an exception to the ideal.[9]

For the Conference the disagreement of community leadership on serious issues of religious life was a novel experience. It seems clear that the Survey and the Canon Law Study generated a certain unease among some members with the orientation renewal might be taking. Objections to Survey conclusions and to the final statement on the revision of canon law did not then coalesce into opposition, however. Indeed, the general membership appears to have been unaware of the rumblings that would later produce a rupture in the organization. By and large, the Conference was caught up in the same energy and sense of possibilities that marked individual communities. And the 95 percent favorable vote of the members on the final report of the Canon Law Committee, *Proposed Norms for Consideration in the Revision of Canon Law* (Washington, D.C.: CMSW, 1968) indicated a solid consensus.

It was the rewriting of the bylaws (1969–71) that sparked the first vigorous public conflict in the Conference. Serious disagreement focused on two areas—the purpose (mission) of the Conference and the structural relation of the Conference to hierarchical authority.

As we have noted in Chapter one, the 1956 statutes of the CMSW defined four main organizational purposes—the promotion of "the spiritual welfare" of sisters in the United States, increased effectiveness in the apostolate, collaboration with other segments of the church, and suitable representation of the interests of sisters to church authorities. Church matters, then, were the field of corporate activity. The revised bylaws, on the other hand, shifted emphasis to the "development of creative and responsive leadership" and to "those forms of service consonant with the evolving Gospel mission of women religious in the world through the Church."

Some members insisted on an amendment to the purpose statement. They urged that the word "spiritual" be inserted to modify "leadership." The modification was not, for them, a matter of semantics but of the very nature of religious life. Conference members were not leaders pure and simple, they argued. They were leaders of communities whose very reason for being was to witness to the spiritual and instill spiritual values into the world. They were chagrined that "the spiritual welfare" of women religious was no longer expressly cited in the new bylaws. Others felt that whatever related to the church in mission was an appropriate concern of all its members, including the sisters. Inserting the word "spiritual" would seem to narrow the presence and mission of the sisters. In fact, it was not desirable. Singling out the spiritual would reinforce dualisms of church and world and of religious and apostolic dimensions at the very moment sisters were struggling to understand their life as one single way.[10]

The second issue was framed by a small group of members as a test of the fidelity and obedience of the Conference to the church. They insisted that the bylaws retain the juridical language of "dependence" on and "submission" to church authority found in the CMSW statutes. Others believed that the connection of the Conference to the church and to its mission was abundantly clear in the statement of purpose and that the earlier language was no longer appropriate in light of Vatican Council positions on the people of God, the dignity of the person, and the equality of the baptized.[11]

Fundamentally, the debates were about the "nature" of religious life and about the source of legitimacy. The new statement of purpose clearly opted for a view of religious life located in and interacting with the world. It linked ministerial activity, including participation in fashioning society, with religious commitment, rejecting the traditional dichotomy between religious life (primary, essential) and the work of ministry (secondary, accidental). In the end the statement of purpose and the bylaws were adopted by large majorities. But the division within the organization was serious and its effects continue to haunt American sisters.

In the next few years controversy mounted in the Conference. It was consistently related to the explosion of change among American sisters. Invariably it reflected sharp differences over the "nature" of religious life and the structural relation between the Conference (therefore, sisters) and the hierarchy, in particular the Vatican. The 1967 remarks of Mary Luke Tobin and Omer Downing, outgoing and incoming presidents, respectively, advert directly to the pervasiveness of conflict among sisters. And in a letter to members Downing lays the rampant confusion at the door of differing interpretations of *Ecclesiae Sanctae*. Quoting her own earlier statement, she says, "Unless we are all talking about the same thing, unless words have the same meaning to all, unless the goals and objectives are clear, and most particularly, unless the means to reach these goals are defined . . . only chaos will result." But those are precisely the conditions that are not possible in eras of cataclysmic change.[12]

Toward the end of the sixties the controversy between the Immaculate Heart sisters and Cardinal McIntyre in Los Angeles became a source of conflict in the Conference. The National Executive Committee's decision to make no public statement on behalf of the Immaculate Heart sisters was contested by several members. They felt not only that the Conference owed the beleaguered women its support but that the outcome of the case held grave implications for all women's communities. In 1968 Cardinal Antoniutti of the Congregation for Religious dispatched a letter to all American communities of sisters.

Criticizing in detail the course renewal was taking in the IHM community, he sternly warned that communities must secure Vatican approval before they could put into effect the changes they were legislating.[13] The letter triggered immense agitation throughout the United States. At the 1969 LCWR Assembly a resolution of support for the IHM community was hotly debated less on the merits of its contents than on whether an affirmative vote signaled disloyalty to the church and disrespect to its officials. When Edward Heston of the Congregation for Religious took the floor to tell the women they must not pass the resolution (and should end the debate), he was followed at once by Angelita Myerscough and Thomas Aquinas (Elizabeth) Carroll, who stated that his intervention was inappropriate and then resumed arguing in support of the resolution.[14] The debate shocked and alienated some members who believed that the Vatican did have the right to control religious life and that the open contradiction of Heston was a direct affront to the authority of the church.

The theme of the 1971 Assembly, *The Church Is for the World*, further fueled the conflict. Just weeks before the Assembly, five members wrote to the president of their dissatisfaction with the planned program. It focused disproportionately, they said, on external deeds (what sisters *do*) rather than on "who we are"—religious women whose proper domain is the spiritual. Direct action for social justice was not fitting for sisters. Several of the writers threatened to stay away from the meeting unless the program was changed.

In 1970–71 a small group of Conference members formed an association called the Consortium Perfectae Caritatis (CPC). Its stated aim was to study *Perfectae Caritatis*, the Vatican II document, and to support one another in the process of "authentic" renewal, that is, renewal in conformity with the directives of the church (as opposed to the aberrations they saw in other communities and in the prevailing positions of the LCWR).[15] In actuality the CPC engaged for years in efforts to supplant the LCWR as the official conference of heads of communities and to discredit it in the eyes of the Vatican and of American bishops. As recently as 1985 a CPC report included a proposal to "establish and extend canonical approval to a new Conference of Major Superiors of Women Religious and permit membership to those congregations only who implement the ESSENTIAL ELEMENTS of the religious life."[16] At first some of the founding women of the new group retained membership in the LCWR. Most, however, eventually severed all ties.

From its inception the CPC espoused a worldview clearly divergent from the one that animates the LCWR purpose statement. Its members understand religious life as having an unchanging nature. CPC literature cites "the pursuit of holiness through the practice of the Evangelical Counsels [that is, poverty, chastity, obedience] as the essential element of religious life." It underscores the "permanent ecclesial commitment" of religious "to a corporate and institutional apostolate under the guidance of the hierarchy and in support of the Magisterium." And it asserts "a clear and unequivocal position" in support of the authority of the hierarchy and its right to regulate religious life.[17]

Coincidentally, just at the time when those members disturbed by the orientation of renewal in the United States were first identifying each other and beginning to coalesce, a second group held a couple of meetings to discuss how they wanted the renewal to move. This self-styled "loose association" was an ad hoc group composed of some thirty persons, heads of men's and women's communities. The participants, people of progressive bent, attended by invitation. The group met in May, 1969, and again in September, 1970. By then the IHM controversy had alarmed many who feared it portended the demise of the change movement. The purpose of gathering was to regroup, so to speak, with a view to formulating some sort of position on preferred directions in renewal.

Although the women who took part in these meetings were members of the LCWR, the group had no structural ties with the conference nor did it represent the Conference. However, at its September, 1970, meeting the "loose association" drafted a statement of principles they believed should guide the renewal process. It included no mention of an essential nature of religious life. Rather, it characterized the purpose of religious life as "to live in harmony with the gospels." Far from being distanced from the world, it declared, the religious community must be "outgoing and open to the secular." And it stated, "Religious must read the culture of the times and create new forms [of service] to respond to the present needs of people. Thus, they provide a dynamic element not locked into the institutional structure that loses in time the capacity for creative innovation and change."[18]

Somehow this statement was circulated at the LCWR National Assembly immediately following the loose association meeting. To the horror of some, for whom the document was a prime exhibit of all that had gone awry in renewal, it apparently reached the floor of the Assembly. Records lead to the inference that the draft was circulated in some more or less organized way—whether for endorsement or simply information is unclear.[19] One informant thinks its introduction was accidental; another remembers it as a deliberate effort to keep everyone informed. There is no evidence whatever that the loose association planned in advance to disseminate the statement in the Conference. There is also no evidence that the group was trying to keep its work secret. There appears to have been some floor debate, in which it became clear that the statement was anathema to some. Although the piece did not represent a Conference position and had not been adopted by its members, evidence suggests that it played a catalytic role in the decision of the women who separated from the Conference to found the CPC. A letter written by Eucharia Malone, SM, to some of the women who were then gravitating toward the group that would become the CPC alludes to what appears to be the loose association draft. She proposes to her addressees that they not attack the statement head on but that she, acting in her own right as an LCWR member, circulate an alternative statement in hopes of getting "more names of major superiors who think as we do." [20]

With the severing of relations between these members and the LCWR the ideological spectrum of the Conference contracted. Conflict has not disappeared from the LCWR, but there is not the polarization of the decade following Vatican II. Rarely, if ever, does conflict center on "the nature of religious life." When Conference members participated in the two religious life studies and the critique of the 1977 draft of canon law, for example, responses were not framed in terms of polar opposites.

Interestingly, resolutions introduced at Assemblies are usually adopted by lopsided majorities. Even in 1971 the much-debated bylaws were adopted by a vote of 356 to 39 with 2 abstentions. The goals formulated by the 1976 National Assembly were accepted by the preponderance of the membership (and, in 1984, reaffirmed with modifications in emphasis). The Corporate Statement of the 1981 Assembly, strongly denouncing the arms race and pledging the women to peacemaking, was unanimously adopted. Evaluations of Conference activity and leadership handling of specific situations garner high approval ratings.[21] And, as recounted in Chapter Two, the women expressed a fairly consistent position on the Vatican document *Essential Elements*, noting quite bluntly that its formulations simply do not reflect the American renewal experience of the past three decades and that many of its central premises are foreign to American sisters.

If questions pertaining to the "nature of religious life" are no longer the source of bitter division, relations with ecclesiastical authority remain an issue about which members are conflicted. Tension, often accompanied by fear, tends to rise when a matter concerns the role of authority as one or the only source of legitimacy.

In 1979, for example, LCWR president Theresa Kane, greeting John Paul II in the name of American sisters, unleashed a furor by directly appealing to the Pope for inclusion of women in all church ministries. Although many who were present, including National Conference of Catholic Bishops president John R. Quinn, vouched for the gentility and respectfulness of Kane's manner, the first reaction of Conference members was mixed. Many applauded her courage,[22] many agreed with her statement but were troubled by its timing, a handful were offended. Five discontinued membership in the Conference. However, when the members reflected together in regional meetings, the prevailing attitude was acceptance of her actions and support of Kane. There was recognition that what she had said was, in fact, truthful and that the church must confront its systemic exclusion and depreciation of women. The National Board discussed the incident and its fallout at length and stood behind Kane. The main issue around which tension materialized was not the content of her remarks but the proper relation of Kane (and of the Conference as a church body) to ecclesiastical authority. If nothing else, Kane violated institutional protocol. In later conversations churchmen informed Kane not only that she should not have said what she did but that it violated protocol for her to insist on approaching the Pope afterward for his blessing. According to "protocol," she was told, the pope determines who gets his blessing. In a subsequent meeting of LCWR representatives with the head of the Congregation for Religious, Cardinal Eduardo Pironio noted gently that if sisters have any questions or criticisms regarding church matters, they should communicate privately with ecclesiastical officials.

Similarly, although the vast majority of the members were offended and outraged when women were turned away from the altar during the National Assembly in 1982,[23] the body could not reach agreement on an appropriate response. Anger and fear were palpable in the room. The sticking point was that the offense had been perpetrated by members of the hierarchy. And the incident involved differing interpretations of rules governing worship. Understandably some members resisted voicing aloud the fact that an action that, on the one hand, struck them as unfair and clearly damaging to the communion of the church stemmed, on the other hand, from the rules and the rigid interpretation of rules by bishops of the church they love. These members felt torn between the conviction that some kind of response was demanded and resistance to any action that might be construed as disloyal to the church. Other members, however, adamantly noted that precisely because the church claims to be a community and consistently preaches justice and the equal dignity of all, it was important that the women be on record against both the incident and the juridical mindset that underlay it.

To understand the change-conflict movement among the sisters themselves is important because it sheds light on the impact of change on those who are changing. It is only part of the account, however. As previous chapters make clear, the changing of American sisters also propelled them into conflict with the men in positions of institutional authority. The relentless criticism, the outright opposition, the public defamation of character visited upon the changing sisters by members of the hierarchy have, in fact, been major constituents of the experience of change. The withholding of approval and encouragement may even have fueled change by forcing the sisters to rely on other sources, including themselves, for validation.

As communities began to act on the mandate for renewal and adaptation, the attitude of Vatican officials toward American sisters began to change. In the first stretch of its history, 1956–66, the LCWR had enjoyed not only the trusting approval of the Vatican but even what may seem to a modern observer to be lavish esteem. Toward the end of the sixties, however, as the direction of change in American communities became clearer, church authorities were manifestly disturbed. The years between 1968 and 1972 saw a string of warnings about deviations from orthodox theories of religious life and firm injunctions that communities must get Vatican authorization in advance for any departures from existing law. In communications to Conference officers or individual heads of communities the Vatican expressed disapproval of the altering of dress, especially when it involved dispensing with a uniform habit, the democratization of community polity, the increased involvement of sisters in public affairs, and, particularly, the growing propensity of women's communities to implement changes without waiting for Vatican approval.

While the LCWR was engaged in the Sisters' Survey, a staff member of the Vatican's Congregation for Religious discreetly sought information on the study. He indicated that officials in Rome were disturbed by the content of various items in the questionnaire but that he hoped to forestall "anything like an official inquiry."[24] As noted in Chapter One, when the Conference president, Thomas Aquinas (Elizabeth) Carroll, presented the new bylaws and title of the Conference to the Congregation for Religious for approval in 1971, she faced the displeasure of officials about the lack of explicit reference to the juridical control of the hierarchy over the Conference and about the change in the name. Although language was quickly incorporated into the document to address the first issue, three years elapsed before the Congregation, persisting in its rejection of the word "leadership," sanctioned the renaming. The 1974 LCWR book *Widening the Dialogue* (Ottawa: Canadian Religious Conference; and Washington, D.C.: LCWR, 1974)[25] angered some Vatican officials, who saw the publication as a deliberate attempt to subvert the credibility of Paul VI's *Evangelica Testificatio*. *Widening the Dialogue* was vigorously attacked by some Vatican officials and by the CPC. As late as 1979 two

Congregation for Religious officials continued to bring up the book as an example of everything objectionable in LCWR. The quasi-official theologian of the CPC, Eileen Masterman, CSC, wrote a scathing critique titled *Widening the Dialogue?* Barbara Thomas recalls Masterman's brandishing the LCWR book indignantly at the 1974 meeting of the two women's groups with Vatican officials. To the CPC the book represented an attack on the "authentic" nature of religious life and, worse still, the intransigence of LCWR before the sanctity of ecclesiastical authority. By the mid-seventies the LCWR's leadership were regularly forced to counter the suspicion, even hostility, of the chief officials of the Congregation for Religious toward Conference programs, publications, speakers, and positions.

For nearly two decades Conference officers have traveled to Rome almost every year to meet with Congregation for Religious personnel. Increasingly elaborate, the preparation for these meetings involves the LCWR representatives and often the full governing board in studying and outlining issues of importance to American sisters. Key recurring topics are ministry, the participation of sisters in efforts for justice, the need for just processes in dealing with persons the Vatican wishes to discipline, sexism in the church, and the dissatisfaction of individual communities with the review of their constitutions. Often they perceive in Vatican officials little real interest in their viewpoints and in the American experience of religious life.[26] Rather, officials take advantage of the occasions to discourse on the iniquities of American religious life and of the Conference and on the correct views that sisters ought to hold regarding subjects on the agenda. In 1980 a group of former LCWR presidents and executive directors gathered for three days to reflect on Conference history. Each was asked to make an audio tape of her recollections of important events and issues during the time of her leadership in the Conference. Independently, and prior to group discussion, every woman who participated in meetings between the Congregation and the LCWR since 1971 described experiences that validate this account. One recalled a Congregation official reading, one after another, a list of objectionable passages he had culled from papers given by Joan Doyle, BVM, and Joan Chittister, OSB, at the 1977 Assembly. Another said, "If you want me to summarize those three hours [of a meeting], . . . I would say we spent our Good Friday that day in November" in the Congregation office. "They expect [LCWR] . . . to have no thoughts of our own but simply to support everything that comes from Rome," offered one. One added, "My faith was shaken many times in those years of struggling with the raw power of those men." [27]

Like the conflict among the sisters, the conflict between Vatican officials and the Conference refers to both the "nature of religious life" and relations with ecclesiastical authority or, more specifically, ecclesiastical authority as the sole source of legitimacy. In the earliest years of renewal, conflict tended to focus on the first issue, although the second issue surfaced almost immediately. American sisters interpreted *Ecclesiae Sanctae* as assigning to each community the responsibility and corresponding authority to determine the path of its renewal. There is absolutely no evidence that sisters deliberately deviated from what they understood to be either basic characteristics of religious life or faithful adherence to the church. In fact, early renewal documents both in the Conference and in communities are studded with quotations from Vatican II decrees and other church documents. They were, therefore, both bewildered and alarmed when reactions from Rome and from a number of American bishops communicated only disapproval and rejection. [28] Many sisters felt betrayed and unjustly castigated when they had worked so hard, often at very high costs, to carry out a mandate of the church. When Vatican officials, in addition to condemning certain changes, began to insist that changes could not be implemented without prior authorization from them, American sisters objected that the renewal process was being prematurely aborted and the lawful autonomy of communities circumvented.[29]

Though its intensity fluctuates, the conflict between LCWR and Vatican officials persists. At times it focuses on issues related to what religious life is. For example, Vatican officials dispute the characterizations of religious identity expressed in the two religious life projects and in inter-American papers. They criticize the involvement of the Conference in social problems and women's movements as incompatible with religious life. They ridicule the very notion of using "lived experience" as a source of knowledge about religious life. On the other hand, LCWR members express their disagreement with the formulations of the 1977 and the final drafts of the code of canon law and of *Essential Elements*. These documents fail, they point out, to incorporate newer theological insights, still less the learning of the past three decades.

In more recent years, however, the emphasis seems to have shifted from the content of religious life to the institutionalized processes that church authorities use to make decisions and exercise power. That theme surfaced even in the seventies, when the LCWR leadership objected to the lack of consultation in the drafting of legislation and statements.[30] The emphasis on process has been far more prominent in the eighties as the Conference has dealt with the way ecclesiastical authority responded in the Mansour and the *New York Times* incidents, the way the Congregation for Religious manages the approval of community constitutions, the way officials intervene in community disagreements, the degree of control that church officials appear to think necessary, and their insistence on the elimination of democratized structures of governance in communities. Over and over, LCWR representatives stress to Vatican officials the critical importance of fair processes particularly when they involve censure and punishment.

For LCWR, persistence in dialogue with institutional

church authority is essential. In evaluations of the annual Conference reports in the early eighties, for example, members gave high marks to the leadership for continuing contact and dialogue with the Vatican and the NCCB. Similar appreciation is consistently voiced from the floor of the Assembly. The women are convinced that the process of transformation among American sisters must continue. They are intent on securing, if not the agreement of official authorities, at least their concession that it is possible to live the American experience of religious life and still adhere to the tradition of the faith. They would not argue that their way of being religious is the only way. They want the various traditions to be upheld—the monastic, the contemplative, the "conventual" pattern preferred by those in the CPC. And, while they do not believe their way of life is accurately described by any of these rubrics, they do not see that as a cause for alarm. They tend to believe that pluralism need not be destructive of communion. They are more inclined these days to suspect that perhaps something new is being born—partly by their choices, partly by forces beyond their control—and that they should allow it to emerge, waiting to name exactly what it is. That conflict would so frequently interweave with change may not have been what American sisters imagined as they set out on their exciting journey three decades ago. Given an option, few would probably have chosen that route. The fact is, however, that the experience of conflict in arenas and with persons who once literally conferred their being upon them has produced qualities of great value. Being right or even being recognized as right no longer matters so much. What is at stake for both individual and community is the quality of fidelity. What is it to be faithful? To whom and to what am I, are we faithful? Scoring points, vanquishing the opposition, or winning seem rather pointless. Maintaining one's dignity, respecting one's piece of the truth, and learning how to be nonviolent in controversy, on the other hand, are worth pursuing.

Sisters are not the only ones the last three decades have schooled in change and conflict. However, theirs is a corporate transformation. As a group, and in a very deliberate way, sisters have undertaken to change collectively. While other groups (national, ethnic, racial, feminist) have sought analogous change, they do not represent persons who freely undertook to live a life that wholly institutionalized their existence. Sisters are a group by choice. The element of "free association," at least as Americans understand it, has played a critical role in transformation. It is as a group that sisters became aware that religious life is actually a *life*. It is not purely a role or a function or profession, though it is all of these. It is not a "state" into whose boundaries they step nor a privileged class in the church. It is precisely a *life*. Sisters are claiming that life and deciding to live it.

Afterword

ALTHOUGH ONE CHAPTER FOCUSES explicitly on the theme, this whole book is, finally, about the rightful coming to power of American sisters. Not the power of office or special status. Most assuredly not systemic power in the Catholic church. Sisters remain institutionally disenfranchised. They are, as they have always been, excluded from the councils where laws are enacted, teachings formulated, judgments rendered. Whatever access they enjoy depends wholly on the good will of the hierarchy; it can be revoked far more easily than it is given. But the sisters are powerful women, nonetheless. They have the power that comes from choosing to be and choosing to know. They have the power that comes from claiming over and over their connectedness with humankind, their roots in the best of American tradition, their name as women, and their responsibility to choose. The book is about connections—new connections and old ones known differently.

If the record is clear about the fact of change, it is not clear about what the future holds for American sisters and religious life. Change is a fascinating thing. As it lures, it transforms, both person and journey, both believer and belief. It is in the questions born of change the sisters will find the vague shapes of the future. For these questions reflect the meanings experience has made possible; they are questions that fifty years ago could not even have been framed. Thus, we bring this book to a close with a few remarks concerning the searchings we believe will continue to engage the energies of American sisters.

Despite their transformed knowing of connection, many sisters experience themselves as disconnected. They seem to be missing a solidarity rooted in some meaning that holds them together precisely as a community. They can't quite name it. Still less do they know how to bring it about. They do understand that their way of life cannot derive its breath from ecclesiastical definitions and regulations, nor even from ecclesiastical blessing. Neither can it arise from their own statements about mission and goals, however carefully forged. Religious life must possess its own inner integrity and authority. It must embody a purpose powerful enough to claim both allegiance and affection.

For a large number of the women, their shared life has to be linked to ultimacy, to the values of the Gospel, to the deepest insights of religious traditions. However named, it must embrace as one single reality both who sisters are and what they choose to stand for together. And, however structured, it must be able to encompass autonomy and relatedness, institution and movement, communal mission and personal dream. It need not make life clear. But it must make life worth living together.

Central to this quest for meaning, we believe, is the identity of sisters as church women. The clear, well-delineated connection with church in which definitions of self were rooted is gone. Were it retrievable, it would not serve. To the degree that creed and polity as well as the attitudes and actions of those who wield institutional authority thwart what sisters believe to be the purpose of their life, they are thrown back on questions of ecclesial identity. A key question is why and whether religious life *as a life* needs the official sanction of church authorities. Is the public, official recognition of a community of women obsolete, a vestige of unwholesome dependence on approval, a by-product of patriarchy? Is it an appropriate practice in a church that teaches that all are called to the fullness of God's life? Is not the life itself and the way it is lived the only authentication needed? Can the church hold self-directed, autonomous women? The questions do not get at the crux of the issue. The truth is that the real question is not yet known.

For some sisters this issue has a special urgency in terms of church structures that seem to violate justice. The apparently needless regulation and control of individuals and communities by ecclesiastical authority seem particularly intolerable. When church policies coerce sisters to speak or act falsely, that is, to repudiate convictions arrived at conscientiously and with care, communities face a moral dilemma. Believing that the demands of the Gospel are as binding on ecclesiastical uses of power as they are on personal choices and behavior, they cannot accept that their submission to ecclesiastical control serves either the mission of the church or the community's fidelity to its original vision. Their very role as public church women, then, places them in an unconscionable position.

If there is to be a future for religious life in this country, we think, officials and sisters must interact forthrightly and imaginatively around these questions. That will exact a different price from each of them. For the hierarchy it will mean giving up dominative ways of governing; for sisters it will entail laying claim to rightful uses of power. For both, it will involve owning that they are peers no matter how distinct their role in the church. Such searching is not a task for sterile spirits. It is a sacred trust. It is a holy work.

Notes

Chapter One

1. Bertrande Meyers, DC, *The Education of Sisters: A Plan for Integrating the Religious, Cultural, Social, and Professional Training of Sisters* (New York: Sheed and Ward, 1941). Meyers studied the efforts of women's religious communities to educate their members prior to World War I and during the post-war period to 1930, concluding that, by and large, the preparation of sister teachers was seriously deficient.

2. Sister Madeleva Wolff (then president of St. Mary's College, Notre Dame), "The Education of Our Young Religious Sisters," paper presented at the National Catholic Education Association, Philadelphia, 1949.

3. Sources for the section on the Sister Formation Conference are unpublished chronologies and outline histories as well as issues of the *Sister Formation Bulletin*, 1955–72. Sister Formation Conference Archives, Marquette University Library, Milwaukee, Wisc.

4. Elio Gambari was on the staff of the Vatican Congregation for Religious. From the late fifties until just after Vatican II he regularly traveled to the United States to lecture to Sister Formation audiences. An enthusiastic, unpretentious man, he made no secret of his admiration and warm affection for American sisters. Joseph Fichter, SJ, is a sociologist. Mary Emil Penet, IHM, justifiably considered the founding genius of the Sister Formation Conference, was its director, 1957–60.

5. *Sister Formation Bulletin* 1 (September, 1954): 3.

6. "Report on the Sister Formation Conference's Vocation Survey," *Sister Formation Bulletin* 3 (Autumn, 1956): 1–7.

7. A more detailed overview of the Sister Formation movement is that of Patricia Byrne in Jay Dolan *et al., Transforming Parish Ministry* (New York: Crossroad, 1989), pp. 133–147. Other sources are cited in Chapter Two, note 8. The ongoing research of Professor Mary

Schneider, OSF, offers probably the most extensive in-depth picture of the SFC.

8. James Tucek, "Priest in Red Cassock," *Voice of St. Jude*, October, 1960, pp. 23–27.

9. Cited in *Sister Formation Bulletin* 2 (March, 1955): 14.

10. Tucek, "Priest in Red Cassock," writing several years later on the occasion of Larraona's appointment as a cardinal, gives him credit for masterminding not only the World Congresses but also three significant papal statements on religious life between 1947 and 1956. Bernard Ransing, who knew and worked with him, told us that Larraona was very close to Pius and strongly influenced his thinking about religious life in general and the life of sisters in particular.

11. At various times in LCWR's history the Congregation has been referred to in different ways: the Sacred Congregation for Religious (SCR), the Sacred Congregation for Religious and Secular Institutes (SCRIS), the Congregation for Religious and Secular Institutes (CRIS), and the Congregation for Institutes of Consecrated Life (CICL). For the sake of simplicity we have used the generic Congregation for Religious throughout.

12. Tucek, "Priest in Red Cassock," p. 26; closing address, Arcadio Larraona, *Proceedings of the Sisters' Section of the First National Congress of Religious of the United States, Notre Dame, Ind.* (Mahwah, N.J.: Paulist Press, 1952), p. 173.

13. Elio Gambari, "Religious Women and the Apostolate in the Modern World," *Sister Formation Bulletin* 5 (Summer, 1959): 1–7.

14. Edward Heston, CSC, letter to Mother Gerald Barry, OP, April 1, 1952, Archives of the Dominican Sisters of Adrian, Mich. (hereafter cited as A/DA).

15. Gerald Barry, letter to heads of all women's communities in the United States, announcing the First National Congress, June 3, 1952, A/DA.

16. Arcadio Larraona, closing address, p. 172.

17. Edward Heston, letter to Gerald Barry, April 17, 1953, A/DA. Heston's account gives credence to Larraona's characterization of the movement for change as "tentative." There seems to have been no long-term, systematic program for bringing about adaptation and organization. Rather officials of the Congregation for Religious proceeded in piecemeal fashion, mandating one strategy at a time.

18. In 1956 the members of the committee were Mother Gerald Barry, OP (the chair); Mother Catherine Sullivan, DC; Mother Eucharista, CSJ; Mother Gertrude Clare, SP; Mother Kathryn Marie, CSC; Mother Marietta, OSU; and Sister Madeleva Wolff, CSC. Barry and Wolff were also members of the original Sisters' Committee. Note: Initials following a person's name identify the community to which he or she belongs. Sisters generally did not use their family surnames in those days, prior to the late 1960s, so complete names are often missing in written records. In this book, the first use of a person's name includes the initials; they may be omitted in subsequent uses.

19. The roster included only the pontifical communities, that is, those under Vatican authority as distinct from diocesan groups under the authority of the local bishop. The organizing committee believed that since the initiative came from the Vatican, only those communities under its jurisdiction could appropriately be invited. They assumed that if the conference was established, diocesan communities would be equally eligible for membership subject to the consent of their bishops.

20. According to the minutes of the meeting Mother Marie, an Ursuline sister, advanced the decisive argument. Archives of the LCWR, Notre Dame University Archives (hereafter cited as A/ LCWR).

21. Although it would be more accurate to use "Conference of Major Superiors of Women" when we refer to the history prior to 1971 and to use "Leadership Conference of Women Religious" for later situations, a number of readers on whom we tested the manuscript found the frequent shift confusing. For the sake of clarity, then, we will use Leadership Conference of Women Religious (LCWR) throughout except where the context makes it necessary to retain CMSW.

22. Bernard E. Ransing, CSC, "Religious and the Holy See," *Proceedings of the Second National Congress of Religious of the United States* (Notre Dame, Ind.: University of Notre Dame Press, 1962).

23. Valerio Valeri, letter to Mother Benedicta, OP, March 25, 1957, A/DA. He notes further the "gift for organization which is characteristic of your great country."

24. National Sisters' Committee, unpublished working paper,

"Summary of Ideas of the Executive Committee on the Formation of a Permanent Conference," September 9, 1956, A/DA.

25. This prior approval was made known to the women at the founding meeting. They thus had advance assurance that the Vatican would sanction their decisions.

26. The Sisters' Survey and the canon law project are discussed in detail in the following chapter.

27. Reporting to the 1967 Assembly, the chair of the Research Committee, Mary Daniel Turner, SNDdeN, offered three committee recommendations, among them that the statutes be revised so that all members could share in policy decisions.

28. Angelita Myerscough, ASC, interview with the authors, July, 1988, A/LCWR.

29. Bylaws of the Leadership Conference of Women Religious, 1972, Article II, sections 1 and 3, A/LCWR.

30. Synod of Bishops, *Justice in the World*, 1971, Rome, in Austin Flannery, OP, ed., *Vatican Council II*, vol. 2 (New York: Costello, 1982), p. 696.

31. This debate is treated at length in Chapter Six.

32. Statutes of the CMSW, mimeographed document, 1956. See the section titled "Subordination of the Conference to the Authorities," A/DA.

33. Literally, "nothing hinders," or "there is no obstacle." This amounts to a certification by official church authority that nothing in a proposed document is at odds with church teaching or discipline.

34. Minutes of the meetings of the LCWR National Board, 1971, A/LCWR.

35. Bylaws of the Leadership Conference of Women Religious, Article II, section 2; Article IX, A/LCWR.

36. Ann Virginia Bowling, interview with the authors, April 25–26, 1988.

37. Mother Alcuin McCarthy, report to the Second General Congress of the States of Perfection, December, 1957, A/LCWR.

38. Angelita Myerscough, unpublished president's report, CMSW internal document, September, 1971, A/LCWR. Myerscough wrote just prior to the Assembly of 1971, which was to change the name of the conference.

Chapter Two

1. Brothers of the Sacred Heart, *Catechism of the Religious Profession*, new edition, (Metuchen, N.J.: Brothers of the Sacred Heart, 1954).

2. The first official codification of church law was mandated by Vatican Council I (1869–70). This work centralized church authority and order. Elio Gambari of the Congregation for Religious observed in 1962 that "those women who were under vows and doing apostolic works at the time of the previous Council [Vatican I] were not religious. They had not yet been admitted to the canonical states of perfection as religious. But now we have a new phenomenon of 1,200,000 religious women enjoying the full canonical state of religion." Opening message at the SFC Leadership Meeting, *Sister Formation Bulletin* 9, no. 1 (Autumn, 1962): 9–10.

3. A typical statement of this orientation is Bernard E. Ransing, CSC, "Religious in the Contemporary Church," a presentation given at the 1968 LCWR Annual Assembly, A/LCWR. Ransing builds a definition of religious life by distinguishing it from both the lay state and the secular institute. The whole presentation proceeds by way of distinctions. He emphasizes that "the religious is separated from the world even if at times he [*sic*] must be in its midst." Ransing argues that religious are juridically, psychologically, and socially separate from the world. He warns against eradicating the distinctions among the states of life in the church even as he voices his appreciation for the universal call to holiness of all Christians.

See also Paul Philippe, OP, "Renewal and Adaptation of Religious Institutes," a paper presented at the LCWR Annual Assembly, August 28–29, 1963, A/LCWR; Thomas E. Clarke, SJ, *LCWR Seminar Papers: Religious Congregations within the Church* (Washington, D.C.: LCWR, 1982), pp. 2–5; Congregation for Religious and Secular Institutes, "Essential Elements in the Church's Teaching on Religious Life as Applied to Institutes Dedicated to the Works of the Apostolate," *Origins* 13, no. 8 (July 7, 1983): 133–42.

4. Elizabeth Carroll, RSM, "Reaping the Fruits of Redemption," in Ann Patrick Ware, SL, ed., *Midwives of the Future* (Kansas City, Mo.: Leaven, 1985), p. 61.

5. *Lumen Gentium*, Chapter 5, article 40: "It is therefore quite clear that all Christians in any state or walk of life are called to the fullness of Christian life and to the perfection of love."

6. *Ibid.*, article 43. Mary Jo Weaver comments on the shift in category. She speaks of sisters becoming "laywomen" and leaving a "quasi-clerical state." She also suggests that they may be defined as laywomen but that they are perceived as "officials within the church." "Inside Outsiders: Sisters and the Women's Movement," in Weaver, *New Catholic Women: A Contemporary Challenge to Traditional Religious Authority* (San Francisco: Harper and Row, 1985), pp. 71–108.

7. On the one hand, these documents seemed to call for a kind of change that would inevitably produce the substantive alteration of religious life. On the other hand, the documents preserved intact the structure of the institution and continued to use the language of traditional paradigms.

8. Mary Schneider, OSF, "The Transformation of American Women Religious: The Sister Formation Conference as Catalyst for Change (1954–1964)," in the Cushwa Center for the Study of American Catholicism, University of Notre Dame, *Working Paper* Series, 17, no. 1 (Spring, 1986). This comprehensive study makes it clear that the SFC was a significant instrument in awakening sisters to their responsibilities in a radically changing world.

See M. Patrice Noterman, "The Evolution and Impact of the Sister Formation Conference 1954 to 1975," paper delivered at the Conference on History of Women Religious, the College of St. Catherine, St. Paul, Minn., June 27, 1989. See also "Survey of a Decade Past . . . Schema for the Decade Ahead," *Sister Formation Bulletin* 10, no. 4 (Summer, 1964): 32–36. This article makes apparent that American sisters were reading major European theologians like Karl Rahner, Yves Congar, Bernard Häring, Leo Suenens, A. Ple, Jerome Hamer, whose sense of history and its integral role in the church's mission distinguished their thinking.

At a colloquium, "Women Religious and the Universal Apostolate," sponsored by Pro Mundi Vita, 1967, Rose Dominic Gabish, SCL (then executive director of the SFC) wrote, "In-service sisters need more than continuous spiritual and professional development. To that they must add insight into modern conditions so that their relations with others may be intelligent and constructive, and their education of youth formative of truly charitable and apostolic men [*sic*] who can translate the words of the Constitution into action. They may not hide their heads in the sands of old routines. The Church in the modern world is not in a separated 'divinized' world, regarding everything outside itself with suspicion, but in a secular, 'hominized' world with many aspects of good on all sides. Sisters cannot afford to make the mistake of Lot's wife, who had a resistance to change and was punished for it." "The Formation of Religious Women of Today," *Pro Mundi Vita* 16 (1967): 37–38.

9. The data from the Sisters' Survey make this evident. So does the first effort undertaken by the LCWR to theorize about religious life, *Widening the Dialogue: Reflection on "Evangelica Testificatio"* (Ottawa: Canadian Religious Conference; Washington, D.C.: LCWR, 1974).

Similarly, "Choose Life" a paper prepared by the National Board of the LCWR and written by Joan Doyle, BVM, for the third inter-American meeting held in Montreal, 1977, A/LCWR highlights the efforts of American sisters to integrate the many aspects of an apostolic vocation. The paper emphasizes the organic oneness of religious life, its fundamental integrity. One looks in vain for language revealing a dualistic worldview that basically structures "reality" by dividing it into two opposing parts and then identifies one of the parts as superior to or more valuable than the other. For example, thinking and feeling are seen as inherently opposed, and the latter judged inferior.

10. Cf. William Butler Yeats, "Among School Children." Is the chestnut tree, the speaker asks, "the leaf, the blossom or the bole?" And "How can we know the dancer from the dance?"

11. In trying to understand the transformation that has taken place in the way American sisters appropriate knowledge, we have been helped by the work of Mary Field Belenky, Blythe McVicker Clinchy, Nancy Rule Goldberger, and Jill Mattuck Tarule, *Women's Ways of Knowing: The Development of Self, Voice, and Mind* (New York: Basic Books, 1986). Their "Introduction" cites the work of William Perry as very important in their own research. For Perry as well as for the writers "knowledge is constructed, not given; contextual, not absolute; mutable, not fixed" (p. 10).

12. Definitions, human constructions, depend on a consensus

among the defined for their longevity. The worldview that definitions impose on "reality" requires the acquiescence of those affected
by the definitions. Definitions and experience do not, cannot, have
a complete and total correspondence. Definitions help make sense
of reality; they do not substitute for experience. When those whose
life is being defined are excluded from the process of designating
its meaning, the definitions, more often than not, distort and even
betray the meaning. In the long run, the excluded begin to take hold
of their responsibility and the right to share in the naming of reality,
especially their own. Globally, over the past thirty years, this has
been more than amply demonstrated. The events that took place in
Eastern Europe in 1990 are a striking example of this fact.

13. *Perfectae Caritatis*, October, 1965.

14. Sister M. Charles Borromeo Muckenhirn, CSC, ed., *The
Changing Sister* (Notre Dame, Ind.: Fides, 1965). This is a collection of
essays dealing with community change. It directly addresses issues
of secularity (sisters vis-à-vis the world).

15. The members of the committee were Charles Borromeo (Mary
Ellen) Muckenhirn, CSC, theologian; Elena Malits, CSC, theologian;
M. Aloysius (Mary) Schaldenbrand, SSJ, philosopher; Jane Marie
Richardson, SL, liturgist; Corita Kent, IHM, artist; Mary Angelica
(Ann) Seng, OSF, social scientist; Jane Marie Luecke, OSB, poet and
educator; Marie Augusta Neal, SNDdeN, sociologist. The Confer-
ence members who served on the committee were Mary Luke Tobin,
SL; Thomas Aquinas (Elizabeth) Carroll, RSM; Mary Daniel Turner,
SNDdeN; Mary Isabel Concannon, CSJ; and Angelita Myerscough,
ASC. These women had degrees in education, history, theology, and
philosophy.

16. Information on the Sisters' Survey comes from the following:
the minutes of the CMSW Research Committee, 1965–67; the reports
of the CMSW Assemblies, 1967–68; the *Proceedings* of the CMSW
Assemblies, 1967–69; and an unpublished interview with the authors
(June 12, 1988) of Marie Augusta Neal, A/LCWR.

For accounts of the research project in its various stages the following articles and book, all authored by Marie Augusta Neal, are
helpful:

"The Relation between Religious Belief and Structural Change in
Religious Orders: Developing an Effective Measuring Instrument,"

Parts 1, 2, *Review of Religious Research* 12, no. 1 (Fall, 1970): 2–16; 12, no. 3 (Spring, 1971): 153–64. These papers were delivered as the H. Paul Douglass Lectures for 1970.

"A Theoretical Analysis of Renewal in Religious Orders in the U.S.A.," *Social Compass* 18 (1971): 7–25.

"Cultural Patterns and Behavioral Outcomes in Religious Systems: A Case Study of Religious Orders of Women in the U.S.A.," in *Religion and Social Change* (Lille: Edition du secretariat, CISR, 1975).

"The Sisters' Survey, 1980: A Report," *Probe* 10, no. 5 (May–June, 1981).

Catholic Sisters in Transition from the 1960s to the 1980s (Wilmington: M. Glazier, 1984).

"American Sisters: Organizational and Value Changes," in *Vatican II and American Catholicism: Twenty-five Years Later*, ed. Helen R. Ebaugh, vol. 2 of *Religion and the Social Order: New Directions in Theory and Research*, ed. David G. Bromley (Greenwich, Conn.: JAI Press, 1991).

17. Neal, "Religious Belief and Structural Change" is a succinct, comprehensive summary of the data from the population study.

18. Neal states this was "the central hypothesis of the study." *Ibid.*, Part 2, p. 153.

19. *Ibid.*, Part 1, p. 13.

20. Marie Augusta Neal, *From Nuns to Sisters* (Mystic, Conn.: Twenty-Third Publications, 1990), n. 9, pp. 126–27. See also Neal, "Religious Belief and Structural Change," Part I, p. 14.

21. Neal summarizes the two belief orientations as follows: "Post-Vatican themes include God acting in history, through people, in ever new ways, and of man [sic] breaking through cultural barriers, ever protesting what is evil while striving to help build structures organized in justice, living as pilgrims, ready to take risks when service to the neighbor calls for this, celebrating this mission together and, through working with people, coming to God. Transforming the world is focal.

"Pre-Vatican themes describe an otherworldly orientation in which God is experienced as remote and/or very personal in family terms. The religious experience calls one out of the world, away from involvement in social issues, where those with a religious calling deal with other people mainly within the confines of places set apart as sacred and look forward to salvation in the afterlife when they have completed their terms of service relatively uncontaminated by the 'world.'" Neal, "Religious Belief and Structural Change," Part 1, p. 154.

22. The members of the committee were M. Antonice Muraski, SSND; M. Magdalen Martin, OP; Ann Marie Kerper, FSPA; J. Charline Shekleton, SDS; Angelita Myerscough, ASC; Timothy Marie Flaherty, OSF.

23. Sources for the study of the first critique of the code of canon law are the minutes and working papers of the Canon Law Committee, 1965–68, A/LCWR; the proceedings of the 1967–68 CMSW Assemblies, A/LCWR; working papers developed by the six CMSW regions, 1966–67, A/LCWR; and an interview from March 11–12, 1988, with Barbara Thomas, one-time chair of the Canon Law Committee.

24. This principle and the other ones cited in this chapter are outlined in the final document presented to the Pontifical Commission, *Proposed Norms for Consideration in the Revision of the Code of Canon Law*, CMSW, 1968. The guidelines can be found pp. 1–7, A/LCWR.

25. *Lumen Gentium*, Chapter 4, article 37.

26. In an interview with Barbara Thomas (March 11–12, 1988) she noted the number of communities that called upon her and other committee members as resource persons to their special chapters or to the community in general. She also spoke of the enormous influence that she believes both the Survey and the Canon Law project had on program planning in individual communities.

27. Joan Chittister, OSB; Lora Ann Quiñonez, CDP; Barbara Thomas; and Mary Daniel Turner.

28. See the report from the study committee, *Journeying . . . LCWR Recommendations: Schema of Canons on Religious Life* (Washington, D.C.: LCWR, 1977), pp. 5–6. There the properties used to critique every canon are listed; namely, the principles of spirituality, individuality, subsidiarity, shared responsibility, equality, and the criteria of clarity, possibility, dynamism, necessity and acceptability. Each principle and criterion is precisely described.

29. See *Journeying . . . LCWR Recommendations*, p. 23.

30. *Ibid.*, p. 11.

31. For example, canon 11.2 pertaining to the establishment of

a house for religious was judged to be too narrowly conceived and to give too much authority to the local bishop. *Ibid.*, p. 16. Similarly, canon 14 was viewed as restricting the legitimate autonomy of a community. *Ibid.*, p. 17.

32. *Ibid.*, pp. 22 and 23.

33. Eighty-nine percent affirmed that the *Schema* should recognize women as mature adults. The following responses also cut across all ages: 84% stated that authority should be understood as to be shared by the total community; 87% agreed that categories used to define religious life should adequately reflect the current realities of the life; 84% supported the emergence of new modes of membership; and 89% favored diversity. *Ibid.*, pp. 28–29.

34. Margaret Ann Leonard, LSA, and Maureen O'Keefe, LSA, *Steps in the Journey: The Contemporary Theology Project, 1976–1979* (Washington, D.C.: LCWR, 1979), pp. 30–43, note that while separation-from-the-world has little currency today among women religious, the actions and language of sisters sometimes stand as a negative judgment on "the world" reflected by some of its cultural values. This the authors view as compatible with the prophetic strain emerging in certain experiences of contemporary religious life. Chapter Three discusses this development more fully.

35. The members of the Contemporary Theology Task Force were Norita Cooney, RSM; Diane Fassel, SL; David Fleming, SM; Margaret Ann Leonard; Jeanne O'Laughlin, OP. They were assisted by Mary Daniel Turner and Lora Ann Quiñonez, in turn, as executive directors. For an overview of the whole process see Lora Ann Quiñonez, ed., *Starting Points: Six Essays Based on the Experience of U.S. Women Religious* (Washington, D.C.: LCWR, 1980), Appendices I and II, pp. 125–37.

36. Both are discussed in Chapter Three.

37. Besides *Steps in the Journey* (1979) and *Starting Points* (1980), the Contemporary Theology Task Force also produced *Resources for the Articulation of a Contemporary Theology of Religious Life* (Washington, D.C.: LCWR, 1977). This booklet contains articles by several specialists, among them Elizabeth Carroll, Sandra Schneiders, IHM, and Arlene Swidler. The Task Force also provided the members with a manual, *Journeying* (Washington, D.C.: LCWR, 1977). It served as a tool for personal reflection in relation to the findings of the project.

38. David Fleming, SM, "Faith Experience of Women Religious Today: A Critical Reflection," *Steps in the Journey*, pp. 46–56.

39. LCWR task force members were Constance Fitzgerald, OCD; Nadine Foley, OP; Janet Mock, CSJ; Anne Munley, IHM; Carmelita Murphy, OP; Marilyn Thie, SC; and Mary Daniel Turner, SNDdeN. The task force was assisted by the staff at the National Secretariat: Rita Hofbauer, GNSH; Margaret Nulty, SC; Lora Ann Quiñonez, CDP; Janet Roesener, CSJ.

40. "Introduction," in Nadine Foley, ed., *Claiming Our Truth: Reflections on Identity by U.S. Women Religious* (Silver Spring, Md.: LCWR, 1988), pp. 1–3 (hereafter cited as *COT*).

41. Anne Munley, "An Explanatory Content Analysis of Major Themes Present in Selected Documents of United States Women Religious," *COT*, pp. 183–91.

42. Religious Life Task Force, "Reflections upon the Religious Life of U.S. Women Religious," *COT*, pp. 173–81. Even the questions used in securing the data were collaboratively formulated by an inter-American committee, and within LCWR they were posed for reflection by various groups.

43. Religious Life Task Force, "Images of God," *COT*, pp. 193–200. In the regions members explored the following questions, "What is our world?" "Who do we say God is?" "Who do we say we are?"

44. Anne Munley, "Note on Process," *COT*, pp. 5–7.

45. Religious Life Task Force, "Reflections upon the Religious Life of U.S. Women Religious," a paper prepared by LCWR for the fifth Inter-American Conference of Religious, 1985, and incorporated into *COT*, pp. 173–81. The Task Force used this paper in its analysis of contemporary thought about and experience of American sisters.

46. The Pontifical Commission appointed to direct the study consisted of Archbishop John R. Quinn, Archbishop Thomas C. Kelly, and Bishop Raymond Lessard.

47. Verbatim recording of LCWR Assembly session, August, 1983, Eastern Audio Associates, Columbia, MD. The tape records not only the statements of the women at the floor mikes but the applause of the other participants, registering broad support for the ideas expressed.

Chapter Three

1. We will not join the perennial debate about whether there is an "American" character. We accept that there are distinctly American traits born out of the Enlightenment. Among them, preferences for equality, for participation in matters that affect one's life, for pluralism and the right to be different, for public dissent and due process are marks of the cultural ethos of this country.

Neither shall we take up the discussion of whether there is *an* "American culture." In one sense, only Native Americans can rightfully claim an indigenous American culture. This country is composed of multiple racial and ethnic groups with their own cultural peculiarities (if not cultures) although the ideal of the "melting pot" has, at certain periods, fostered homogeneity rather than cultural pluralism. In the course of its history, the United States has evolved a set of values, symbols, and institutions that constitute a culture that can legitimately be called "American."

2. This was especially true of communities whose origins or headquarters were in Europe. Even the native communities, however, took on a European cast through their clerical advisors or the rules modeled on those of older communities and approved by the Vatican.

3. Reports of 1958 meetings of the Eastern and Midwestern regions of the CMSW, A/DA.

4. Bernard E. Ransing, remarks to the CMSW National Assembly, St. Louis, Mo., September, 1969, A/LCWR.

5. Marie Augusta Neal noted that "some place along the line, change has occurred and a recognition that a new kind of orientation is needed in administration and training personnel has been absorbed by many orders and is already operating." CMSW press release, April 26, 1968, Archives of the Sisters of Loretto, Nerinx, Ky.

6. Report of meeting of major superiors, January 12, 1960, Washington, D.C., A/DA.

7. Mary Luke Tobin, interview with the authors, December 1–2, 1988, A/LCWR.

8. *Gaudium et Spes*, no. 1.

9. Some commentators believe that, in fact, sisters have too uncritically absorbed the values of American culture. They charge that

the same thoughtless consumerism and unbridled individualism, for example, that pervade broader society have infected the convent to the detriment of the very ends sisters claim to pursue. That such a "shadow side" exists in American culture (as in all others) we don't deny. Sisters are not immune to these. On the whole, however, we believe that the overall effect of the enculturation of religious life in the United States is healthy. We observe many sisters and communities calling themselves and one another to account on the more troubling features of the culture.

10. In probing the meanings of "political," etymology is instructive. The linguistic ancestors of the word include Greek and Latin roots for citizenry, city. "Public" also originates in Latin terms for people. "Political" points to city not primarily as place but as the collective citizenry for whom a given commonwealth (public welfare) has meaning and will be beneficial. And, finally, "welfare" is of Middle English derivation: *wel* + *faren*—that is, good + to go, to travel. The metaphor of "faring" collectively is an appealing one to describe the interacting of a people.

11. In a meeting with American contemplative sisters, Edward Heston of the Congregation for Religious referred to a previous rather heated discussion among the contemplatives, several priests, Cardinal Terence Cooke, and himself. Only in the United States, Heston observed, could a frank, spirited discussion and expression of differences take place with all persons still having the same purpose, the same goals. Minutes of the meeting, September 24, 1969, Archives of the IHM Sisters, Monroe, Mich. (hereafter cited as A/IHM).

12. Letter of Valeri to Mother Gerald Barry, October 9, 1956. The Ransing statement appears in the CMSW Executive Committee minutes, August 24–25, 1958, A/LCWR.

13. At the same time the decision of the organizing committee to structure the Conference regionally rather than nationally was dictated in part by the "variety of customs and laws, state and national" throughout the country as well as the need of sisters to attend to issues pertinent only to certain geographic sections.

14. Mimeographed reports and memos of the First National Congress of Religious of the U.S.A. and of the CMSW, A/DA.

15. See Mother Alcuin McCarthy, unpublished report to the Second General Congress of the States of Perfection, CMSW internal document, December, 1957, A/LCWR.

16. Larraona's comment is found in his evaluation of the 1952 National Congress of Religious in the US, 1956, A/DA. Valeri wrote to Mother Benedicta, April 3, 1956, A/LCWR. Myerscough's account is in the CMSW president's report, September, 1971, A/LCWR.

17. Mother Antonice, SSND, chair of the Canon Law Committee, noted that the law of the church should take into account cultural differences and needs. Specifically, European practices and patterns should not dictate the way of life in other countries. "The beauty of the Church is marred wherever uniformity is mistaken for unity." Letter to "Reverend Father" [no name], March 25, 1965, A/LCWR.

18. Sociologist-priest John Bourg, SJ, delivered the paper "A Sociologist Looks at the Theological Implications of the Sisters' Survey" and theologian-priest Thomas E. Clarke, SJ, presented the paper "The Spirit's Gift: Freedom for the World" at the September, 1968 CMSW National Assembly. Bourg stated that the most important gift women religious could give the church was to be religious as modern, "plural" (that is, diverse and varied) American women. *Proceedings of the CMSW National Assembly*, 1967 and 1968, A/LCWR.

19. Elise Krantz, interview with Quiñonez, October 20, 1988. Krantz, a member 1961–73, was part of the small group who became disaffected enough to break away from the Conference and found a rival organization, the Consortium Perfectae Caritatis. That story is told in Chapter Six.

20. Ann Virginia Bowling, IHM, interview with the authors, April 25–26, 1988.

21. During the same period sisters at large were also organizing to pursue these ends. In May, 1969, a national gathering of sisters drew sixteen hundred to Chicago. They passed eleven resolutions with a social orientation, explicitly stating that sisters could not be silent on contemporary issues like the arms race, racism, and labor practices. Report of Mother Omer Downing to CMSW members, A/LCWR. Out of this meeting grew the National Association of Women Religious, of strong activist bent. The National Black Sisters Conference, Sisters NETWORK (a lobby to influence Congress on domestic policy), and Las Hermanas, all came into being within those few years.

22. Bowling, interview, April 25–26, 1988.

23. As chairperson of the Research Committee, Turner spoke to the Special Assembly of 1970 of the significance of organizational re-

structuring. *Proceedings of the Special Assembly*, A/LCWR. In an October 12, 1970 letter to the members the president, Angelita Myerscough, quoted Turner's words to underscore her own view of the potential of the newly reorganized Conference for social justice, A/LCWR.

24. The earliest reference explicitly linking American cultural values and religious identity and mission is a negative one. The clearest Conference references point to those cultural traits the sisters must weed out of their own identity and eradicate in social structures.

25. In her remarks to the Assembly Margaret Brennan, a candidate for office, related religious life to the gift of prophecy. As such it was meant to be revelatory of God's message to Moses, "I have heard the cries of my people in their affliction and oppression, and I have a mind to set them free" (Exod. 3:7). Religious communities, she said, were being called to refound themselves in their original spirit to witness among the poor, the oppressed, those most burdened by the consequences of sin. Minutes of the business meeting, September, 1971, A/LCWR.

26. In the fall of 1978 the Contemporary Theology Task Force asked the regions to discuss linkages between culture and religious life. A substantial number perceived a negative mutuality between the two; a smaller number believed a positive mutuality is possible; an even smaller group thought there is no connection (working papers of the Contemporary Theology Task Force, A/LCWR). See Chapter 2, note 34.

27. See Chapter Two.

28. Cardinal Antoniutti, letter to Mother Omer Downing, SC, February 16, 1968, A/LCWR.

29. Margaret Brennan, interview with the authors, May 6–7, 1988. Asked whether she was conscious *at the time* of a degree of anti-Americanism, she replied, "Absolutely, absolutely. Even from other nuns, from other groups of sisters [in international forums]."

30. Bowling, interview, April 25–26, 1988. The letter originated with the head of the Congregation for Religious, Cardinal Antoniutti, who wrote to Vatican ambassadors around the world. In the United States the ambassador recast the letter (January 28, 1972) and sent it to the NCCB, whose president, Cardinal John Krol, decided to circulate it to all the bishops. According to records of a meeting between

LCWR's executive committee and the president of the UISG in 1972, only in Spain and the United States did the Vatican representative transmit the correspondence to the local hierarchy.

31. Minutes of the LCWR National Board, September 3, 1972, A/ LCWR.

32. A series of Vatican interventions into the internal life of women's communities occurred in rapid succession between 1982 and 1984. In some cases—and in reference to the LCWR—what the Vatican found objectionable related to the social involvement (in Vatican parlance, "social insertion") of American sisters. Indeed, between 1983 and 1985 LCWR pursued the issue of sisters and politics in an effort to secure Vatican acceptance. The appeal to American mores and expectations was a critical aspect of this work.

33. Carroll, RSM, was president in 1971–72.

34. LCWR Executive Committee, letter to Augustine Mayer, August 3, 1972, regarding Protocol 194/72. The letter further questions whether the Congregation for Religious is able to perceive "women as adults—as capable of reflecting upon their lived experiences and relating these experiences to the jurisprudence offered by the church." A/LCWR.

35. Again, although the Pope's letter to the American bishops applied the "pastoral service" to male as well as female communities, LCWR leadership had learned early in 1972 that the real concern was about the women and that the Vatican was considering an investigation of their communities. Bette Moslander, CSJ, and Lora Ann Quiñonez protested strongly, reminding others present of the public storm that an initiative aimed solely at the women would generate. It was the experience of LCWR members in the various regions that the male religious tended to absent themselves from dialogues with the bishops. The bishops themselves, during NCCB meetings, confessed that the men "did not seem to be interested." In some areas men religious remarked publicly that the study was really aimed at the women.

Chapter Four

1. Charles Paul Freund, "The Power of, and behind, a Name," *Washington Post*, February 7, 1989.

2. The second largest group of "religious," that is, the priests, have generally tended to think of themselves as "clergy" rather than "religious." Unordained male religious, the brothers, were relatively few in number and generally not very visible or held in high esteem (many viewed them as men who lacked what it took to enter the "higher" state of priesthood). The upshot was that in the decades preceding Vatican II the sisters, for all practical purposes, inhabited a middle state that, while it did not elevate them to the rank of clergy, did essentially remove them from the lay state.

It should be noted that these women did not belong to the *canonical* category "religious" until 1900. Prior to that time church authority did not accept their form of life as appropriate for "religious." Then, as now, experience outran legal definitions. In their own mind (and in the mind of the people) the sisters seemed not to doubt that their life was "religious life."

3. Typical statements of Catholic officials, for example, launch forth with a vigorous assertion that women are equal to men. Then comes the qualifier—*but* "equality does not mean sameness." Usually there follow solemn pronouncements and exhortations about women's "particular" *nature* and its essential link with motherhood. Neither of us is inclined to disparage mothers and motherhood. It continues to astound us, however, that at least official Catholic voices do not utter similar definitions about the "particular" nature of men and its essential link with fatherhood.

4. Our use of phrases like "the women of LCWR" or "the members as a collectivity" does not mean that the same group of persons has remained in place over a quarter of a century. Because membership eligibility is tied to specific leadership roles, the makeup of the Conference is, as a matter of fact, unusually fluid as organizations go. As communities elect new leadership, Conference membership turns over. We are speaking, rather, of the cumulative impact of many women over many years. The mission of the Conference and the areas it consistently addresses in its goals as well as a degree of stability in structures (the National Assembly, regional activities, the yearly succession of the presidency, the Board, the Secretariat) make for continuity of emphases.

5. The annotated draft is among Mother Barry's papers (A/DA). Mary Philip Ryan, OP, the community historian of the Adrian Do-

minicans, who knew Barry, told us the writing is not Barry's. She thought it might be that of her assistant, on whom Barry often relied for advice.

6. Several years earlier Mother Barry, explaining the decision to have a panel of four sisters address "Modern Comfort and Convenience in the Light of Religious Spirit" at the First National Congress of Religious, added, "Why should any man tell us about our comforts and conveniences?" *Time*, August 25, 1952. Yet most of the theoretical papers at the Congress were presented by men. It would have been extremely unlikely for any sister to assume theological expertise then.

7. Pope Paul VI, quoted by Mary Luke Tobin in her foreword to the proceedings of the 1964 CMSW National Assembly, A/LCWR.

8. Ann Virginia Bowling, interview with the authors, April 25–26, 1988. The idea of changing the name, added Bowling, had been discussed by the National Board for several months in advance. The membership was asked to send in suggestions to be presented to the 1971 Assembly.

9. And not until 1982—ten years after the members had voted to adopt it—was the new title listed in the *Annuario Pontificio*, a worldwide directory of Catholic officials, religious communities, and organizations published annually by the Vatican. Until that year the *Annuario* doggedly retained the old name. The women, meanwhile, did not wait for formal approval to begin using their new name, a fact that did not escape the notice (and the ire) of Archbishop Augustine Mayer, then second in command in the Congregation for Religious, who saw it as "disobedience." He continued to bring the topic up at meetings well into the 1980s.

10. Margaret Brennan, Theresa Kane, Francine Zeller, Joan Chittister were presidents of LCWR. Mary Daniel Turner was its executive director from 1972 to 1978; Ann Virginia Bowling was on the staff from 1971 to 1976. All the events alluded to occurred between 1972 and 1979.

11. These often seemed motivated by fear of offending—worse yet, hurting—individual clergy and bishops. Another thread in cautionary statements was that "our" problems are so minor compared with the sufferings of the poor, minorities, and the victims of torture and ought to be set aside so that energies can go to victims of real op-

pression. In later years, as the women began to comprehend that the Catholic church's official definitions of Jesus' maleness, priesthood, authority, and jurisdiction and the theologies underlying them are part of what the hierarchy defines as essential to the very nature of the church, more women understood that claiming their identity as women would put them in opposition to the institution that, for many, is the essential source of validation for their being and life as sisters. This realization intensified the fear of rupture.

12. Thomas Aquinas (Elizabeth) Carroll, letter to Bishop James Hogan, November 16, 1971, A/IHM (Monroe).

13. Margaret Brennan and Paul Boyle, joint report to the memberships of CMSM and LCWR, mimeographed document, A/LCWR.

14. Report of the meeting of religious women with the special bishops' commission, May 2–3, 1968, A/LCWR.

15. A number of studies make clear that talking plays a critical role in women's maturing. Linguist Deborah Tannen, author of *That's Not What I Meant* (New York: Ballantine, 1986) and *You Just Don't Understand* (New York: William Morrow, 1990), says that women tend to use conversation to establish, maintain, and nurture relationships; men, to transmit information. For women conversation is an opportunity for exploring the other's world, her feelings, the connections among persons in the dialogue. Carolyn Heilbrun, author of *Writing a Woman's Life* (New York: Norton, 1988), sees women's talk as the major means for awakening women to the public and systemic meanings of their personal experience; talking is the forum in which women generalize from their private knowledge and recognize it in relation to the knowledge of others. *Women's Ways of Knowing* (New York: Basic Books, 1986) by Mary Field Belenky, Blythe McVicker Clinchy, Nancy Rule Goldberger, and Jill Mattuck Tarule demonstrates the seminal role of language and speech in the intellectual and moral development of women. Language supplies the tags and the frameworks through which women gain access to their own experience and connect it both to the experience of other persons and the systematized experience of humanity. Suzette Haden Elgin's science fiction novel *Native Tongue* (New York: DAW Books, 1984) creates an imaginary world in which the women expend immense energy to develop a language of their own whose words and structures enable them to give voice to ideas not possible in present language systems.

Their language allows them to perceive facets of reality rendered invisible or obscured by the standard language of the realm and, thus, to have new thoughts. Their venture has to be kept secret from the men, for it is a subversive act punishable by annihilation.

16. Bowling, interview, April 25–26, 1988.

Chapter Five

1. The term is used by Anne E. Patrick, SNJM, "The Moral Decision-maker: From Good Sisters to Prophetic Women," unpublished address to the LCWR National Assembly, New Orleans, September 2, 1985, A/LCWR.

2. The phrase "Mapping Their Moral Domain" is taken from *Mapping the Moral Domain: A Contribution of Women's Thinking to Psychological Theory and Education*, ed. Carol Gilligan *et al.* (Cambridge, Mass.: Harvard University Press, 1988).

3. The fact is that in the decades between the admission of apostolic communities into the canonical category of "religious" and the rearrangement of relationships (in practice if not in law) triggered by Vatican II sisters and their congregations were defined and regulated in terms of dependence and submission. That is, the perception of oneself as dependent and subordinate was inherent in the legal and theological formulas of the vows and of religious consecration. And the discipline, the lived practice, structured such dependence and subordination into approved behavior patterns.

4. In many communities preparation for and implementation of chapters was clearly an experience of initiative, self-determination, the ability to choose directions. Individuals and communities tasted a level of power and self-mobilization utterly unprecedented in the history of religious life. Overnight sisters, simply by deliberation and choice, brought about momentous changes. Overnight they were compelled to take responsibility for decisions previously reserved to persons in positions of authority. Overnight they were challenged to assume their share of responsibility for framing and acting on the mission of the community and for insuring the common good of both church and world. Overnight old structures dissolved and bases of institutional power reconfigured. Since then communities have held

to a fairly steady course of reidentifying their corporate spirit and charting their mission. They continue to invent and fine tune the structures of corporate choice-making. They continue to believe that the world is an appropriate forum for their involvement.

5. See Chapter Two.

6. The two critiques of the code of canon law as well as the varied resolutions adopted at the National Assemblies over the years provide rich materials in this regard. A monograph, *The Corporate Response: Why and How*, ed. Rita Hofbauer, GNSH (Silver Spring, Md.: LCWR, n.d.), is an example, among many, of the resources LCWR offered sisters for taking responsibility for the norms that inform their choices.

7. "Procedures for Due Process" discusses the need for due process within the religious community and suggests structures. "Issues of Separation" deals with the separation of a member from the community and, again, offers recommendations for processes to make separation more just and less painful. Monographs by LCWR Church Law Committee (Washington, D.C.: LCWR, 1972 and 1974, respectively).

8. See minutes of the National Assembly, 1986, A/LCWR.

9. The Consortium is discussed in Chapter Six. See in particular the minutes of the meeting held in Rome, November, 1974, between LCWR and CPC representatives and the Congregation for Religious, A/LCWR.

10. This phrase occurs in the introduction of *Justice in the World*, the statement of the 1971 synod of bishops. In its entirety the sentence, often cited by American sisters, reads: "Action on behalf of justice and participation in the transformation of the world fully appear to us as a constitutive dimension of the preaching of the Gospel or, in other words, of the church's mission for the redemption of the human race and its liberation from every oppressive situation."

11. A review of the minutes of meetings between LCWR officers and church officials between 1972 and 1990, both in the United States and in Rome, reveals how many times and in how many different circumstances LCWR representatives spoke of these values as essential to the religious consecration and mission of sisters.

12. "The Moral Decision-maker" by Anne E. Patrick and "From Moral Insight to Moral Choice" by Margaret Farley are attached to

the official minutes of the 1985 LCWR National Assembly, A/LCWR.

13. The official position of the NCCB was that responsible evaluation of candidates required consideration of a whole range of issues, including but not limited to abortion. Their statement cited a number of both domestic and foreign policy issues that were important.

14. These were, respectively, Margaret Cafferty, PBVM; Miriam Therese Larkin, CSJ; Catherine Pinkerton, CSJ; and Lora Ann Quiñonez.

15. Both men were distressed about canceling out. Left to their own devices, they might have made other choices. At the time they believed that their institutional roles would be undermined if they attended the Assembly. New Orleans Archbishop Phillip Hannan became the celebrant at the liturgy. An LCWR member went as an emissary to explain the situation to Hannan, making very clear to him why Quinn and Laghi had withdrawn and why the Conference leadership would not disinvite Farley. Hannan not only agreed to celebrate the liturgy but was gracious, warm to the Assembly.

16. See in particular "Reflection on NYT/CRIS," a paper given by Helen Amos, RSM, at the 1985 National Assembly. Amos, at the time head of the Sisters of Mercy, spoke to the dilemmas this event brought in its wake. She analyzed the "contest" and the "contestants." She posed a series of telling questions; for example, "What precise mixture of challenge and support does the signer need? What is the preponderating need of the church in its role as servant of truth? What of the particular needs of the US church? How much weight ought one place on the church's need for true dialogue on a desperately troubling issue of enormous social as well as personal impact?" Archives, Sisters of Mercy of the Union, Silver Spring, MD.

17. See "Claiming Our Power as Women in the Midst of Political Struggle," an expanded version of a paper delivered by Maureen Fiedler, SL, at a conference titled Women Church: Claiming Our Power, Cincinnati, October, 1987.

Chapter Six

1. Marie Augusta Neal, *Catholic Sisters in Transition* (Wilmington: M. Glazier, 1984). The raw numbers continued to rise. The rate of

increase, however, slowed and began to decline in the early 1950s—
a fact that seems to have eluded general notice.

2. *Ibid.*, tables V, Va, Vb.

3. *Ecclesiae Sanctae*, paragraph 3.

4. The Sisters' Survey did not initiate individual community
change. In her report to the 1968 CMSW Assembly, Neal noted that
41% of the communities had begun structured planning for chapters
before the release of *ES* (1966), which antedated the Survey. It did
spur some communities to address change. And it certainly impacted
many of the special chapters. Neal was frequently invited to address
chapters. And the computer printouts of national and individual data
from the Survey were major resources in constructing proposals and
rationales.

5. The categories are discussed at length in Chapter Two. This
facet of Survey findings is the topic of Neal, "Cultural Patterns and
Behavioral Outcomes in Religious Systems: A Study of Religious
Orders of Women in the U.S.A.," in *Religion and Social Change* (Lille:
Edition du secretariat, CISR, 1975). In another article, "The Relation
between Religious Belief and Structural Change in Religious Orders:
Developing an Effective Measuring Instrument," Part I, *Review of
Religious Research* 12, no. 1 (Fall, 1970): 2–16, Neal notes, "Religious
beliefs as held by the members play significant roles in the process of
structural change in religious communities. The attachment of some
persons to existing structures is defined by them in religious terms as
is also the willingness of others to give up these same structures and
to introduce new ones. Holding certain religious beliefs predicts resistance to certain structural changes. Holding other religious beliefs
predicts readiness for change."

6. Marie Augusta Neal, interview with the authors, June 12, 1988.
Neal seemed genuinely surprised when the authors raised the question.

7. Neal, "Religious Belief and Structural Change," Part II, p. 154.

8. Subsequently the fourth theologian wrote to Neal advising
caution in the use of the terms.

9. Proceedings of the 1967 CMSW Assembly, A/LCWR.

10. The debate illustrates an important point of Neal's analysis of
the Sisters' Survey. She noted that the sisters who preferred change
also showed a marked preference for newer theologians (for ex-

ample, Karl Rahner, Henri de Lubac, Hans Küng, Johannes Metz). And a major distinction between these and older theologians was "an emphasis on the 'this-worldly' as distinct from the transcendent." (Suhard, 1946. Cited by Neal in "The Relation between Religious Belief and Structural Change in Religious Orders: Developing an Effective Measuring Instrument," Part I, *Review of Religious Research* 12, no. 1 [Fall, 1970], p. 10.) This-worldliness was not seen as a secular stance. Rather it located religious belief and commitment within the concrete situations of history.

11. The terms of this debate are laid out in the following records: minutes of the CMSW Eastern Regional Meetings, October 16, 1969, and December 1, 1969; "The Philadelphia Response to the Booz, Allen, Hamilton Report," unsigned, undated attachment to the October minutes; and working papers of the CMSW Special Assembly, February 23–25, 1970, A/LCWR. A copy of the "Philadelphia Response" among the papers of Alice Anita Murphy, SSJ, bears handwritten annotations by her dating the piece October, 1969, and identifying it as a compilation of the thinking of four Philadelphia major superiors. Archives of the Sisters of St. Joseph, Chestnut Hill, Pa. (hereafter cited as A/SSJ).

12. Omer Downing, letter to members of the CMSW, March 15, 1968. The Tobin and Downing observations were made at the 1967 CMSW National Assembly. See the Proceedings, A/LCWR.

13. April 9, 1968, A/LCWR.

14. Angelita Myerscough, interview with the authors, July 14–15, 1988.

15. Claudia Honsberger, IHM, in "The Reform of Renewal," an unpublished paper delivered to the Consortium, January 25, 1971, expresses the sentiments of these women. Honsberger, then a member of the LCWR and a very influential founder of and continuing power in the CPC, reveals her profound disenchantment with the direction of renewal. Renewal was meant to be, she says, a deepening of fervor, sacrifice, prayer, and the sense of apostolate. Prayer, works of penance, the example of their lives were the major instruments that sisters had for attaining the objectives of Vatican II. Religious life is a defined state with essential elements: consecration by vow to Christ, common life, common prayer, common habit, and community commitment. She acknowledges that changes

were needed: "formalisms, depersonalization and authoritarianism, where they existed, had to be replaced by a new concept of authority." But the wholesale abandonment of essential elements of the life which ensued was never intended. She juxtaposes against contemporary culture—materialistic, sex-ridden, permissive—the example of austerity, self-control, obedience, womanly dignity, and voluntary poverty to which religious are called.

16. *Consortium Perfectae Caritatis*, mimeographed document, August 25, 1985.

17. Sources consulted for information on CPC positions include *What Is the Consortium Perfectae Caritatis?* (mimeographed brochure, 1979, revised 1985); *Strain Forward* (March–April, 1971); *Consortium Perfectae Caritatis* (March, 1971; May–June, 1971; September–December, 1971); notes from press interviews with John Hardon and with John Mole; papers delivered at Consortium meetings by Claudia Honsberger ("The Reform of Renewal," January 25, 1971; and "Religious Life Today: Ecclesial Nature," March 1, 1971); an undated, unsigned paper purporting to "report" on the LCWR Assembly of 1971 and apparently circulated among people critical of LCWR; and a letter of James A. Viall, chairman, CPC, to Cleo S. Schmenk, February 14, 1970, A/LCWR.

An invaluable resource for analyzing the differences among the worldviews and concepts of religious life is the verbatim proceedings of a meeting of representatives of the Congregation for Religious, the CPC, and the LCWR, November 12–14, 1974, A/LCWR.

18. Mimeographed paper, September, 1970, A/LCWR.

19. Since the group had no official organizational base, any memos or reports it might have produced were not deposited in corresponding institutional files. The authors probed the topic with a number of informants, but their recollections are hazy and differ in some details. Information is sketchy.

20. Eucharia Malone, SM, letter of November 28, 1970, to Alice Anita Murphy, CSJ, A/SSJ. According to CPC records the Consortium "was brought into being at the LCWR meeting held in St. Louis in September, 1970, when some of the major superiors—who, incidentally, had never met before—became alarmed at the direction the assembly was taking. During the remaining days of the conference, these concerned major superiors formed a group which decided to

do something positive to offset the continuing problems which they foresaw." CPC, *What Is the Consortium Perfectae Caritatis?* p. 2. In an interview with one of the authors in October of 1988, Elise Krantz, a founding member and the current president of the CPC, told of the dismay of these members and their sense of urgency to halt what they saw as the disintegration of religious life. The group met formally on December 2, 1970.

21. See, for example, membership responses to the Conference reports of 1983–90. Those were years of acute tensions between Vatican authorities and the Conference in the context of the liturgical fiasco of the San Francisco Assembly, the ouster of Agnes Mansour from her community, the string of interventions in individual communities (somewhat reminiscent of the "apostolic visitations" of the late sixties), the release of the *Essential Elements* and the papal initiative directed at American communities, the *New York Times* statement, and the inclusion of Farley as an Assembly speaker. Invariably members' approval of Conference programs and the leadership's actions was in the 80–95% range. When it dropped to the 75% mark, the weight of responses shifted to "uncertain" rather than "disapprove." Such responses were frequently accompanied by a comment that the person was new and not well enough informed to judge. A/LCWR.

22. The content of Kane's remarks was hardly radical. The novelty lay in the fact that her words were voiced publicly to the supreme ecclesiastical authority of the Catholic church. Indeed, during that first papal visit to the United States, Kane was the only American given a public forum. As a nun, she should, according to one worldview, have exuded deference and docility. As a woman in an ecclesiastical system in which women have no juridical standing, she was there purely on the sufferance and good will of the men in charge. No matter how mild the content, therefore, it took courage, symbolically and emotionally, to utter it.

23. The incident is described in Chapter Four.

24. Letter from Bernard Ransing to Rose Emmanuella Brennan, SNJM, April 23, 1967, A/LCWR. "Objections," Ransing said, "can be and are being made to a goodly number of the questions, the way they are stated, the fact that there is no *one* answer to some of them" (emphasis added). He advised against giving any publicity to

the study. "I do know that It [Congregation for Religious] would be displeased if publicity were given, or even, which is more likely, if there are any major leaks."

25. As noted in Chapter Two, this was the earliest Conference venture into describing and interpreting religious life from new perspectives.

26. This is not true of Jean Jadot and Pio Laghi, the Vatican's representatives in the United States, 1973–1990. These officials met with LCWR leadership at least twice yearly, more often during crises. They seemed relatively interested in the American church, including religious communities. Generally they were fair. During some critical moments they offered useful advice and sought to ameliorate Vatican initiatives.

27. Report of the 1980 meeting of former LCWR presidents and executive directors, A/LCWR. Other former presidents voiced similar perceptions; interviews with authors: Margaret Brennan, May 6–7, 1988; Margaret Cafferty, April 17, 1988, and December 15, 1988; Helen Flaherty, SC, December 4, 1988; Bette Moslander, CSJ, May 16–17, 1988; Barbara Thomas, March 11–14, 1988. A/LCWR. Minutes of the meetings between LCWR and Congregation for Religious representatives in 1979, 1982, 1985, 1986 are also sources, A/LCWR.

28. We must note, however, that there were exceptions. A handful of American bishops risked the disapproval of their colleagues by publicly defending the sisters and stating their trust in the women's faith and commitment to the church. Joseph Breitenbeck and Maurice Dingman were steadfast allies in the early years.

At the request of CMSW president Mary Luke Tobin, the conference of bishops in the United States initiated regular contacts with LCWR in 1966. At least officially, NCCB presidents and general secretaries, particularly in the past decade, have dealt fairly with LCWR officers and executives. They have sometimes used their influence with the Vatican or with individual American bishops on behalf of LCWR. The majority of bishops who served on the NCCB committee for liaison with LCWR were genuinely interested in religious communities and took LCWR's concerns seriously. Most were personally warm as well.

Certainly John R. Quinn, as head of the commission named by the Pope in 1983 to assess American religious life, discharged his mandate evenhandedly and justly. In 1985 and 1986 he accompanied LCWR representatives during their annual meeting with Congregation for Religious officials. His presence was invaluable.

29. See the letters of Thomas Aquinas (Elizabeth) Carroll to Omer Downing and the Executive Committee, February 12, 1968, to Paul VI, March 19, 1968, and to Ildebrando Antoniutti, September 14, 1971; the proposed recommendations of LCWR to the Congregation for Religious, mimeographed document, September 13, 1970; a report of the meeting of the LCWR Executive Committee with Mary Linscott, SND, president of the International Union of Superiors General, April 28, 1972. All these papers are in A/LCWR.

30. Even earlier, on April 29, 1968, Rose Emmanuella Brennan wrote to Ransing: "Most of all, I think, the American sisters desire greater openness in communication with the hierarchy and the Sacred Congregation; and especially that there be a two-way line so that there can be more representation by them in advance of decisions." A/LCWR.

Church Documents Cited

1964

Lumen Gentium (LG): Vatican Council II dogmatic constitution on the church

1965

Perfectae Caritatis (PC): Vatican Council II decree on the renewal of religious life

Gaudium et Spes (GS): Vatican Council II pastoral constitution on the church in the modern world

Dignitatis Humanae (DH): Vatican Council II declaration on religious freedom

1966

Ecclesiae Sanctae (ES): Vatican norms for the implementation of *Perfectae Caritatis*

1969

Renovationis Causam (RC): Vatican instruction concerning the renewal of religious life, especially in reference to formation programs

Venite Seorsum (VS): Vatican instruction on the renewal of contemplative communities

1971

Evangelica Testificatio (ET): Papal exhortation to apostolic (active) religious communities

1975

Evangelii Nuntiandi (EN): Exhortation by Paul VI on evangelization in the modern world

1983

Essential Elements (EE): Compilation of Vatican teachings on apostolic religious life

Index